A guide to the world of German Romantic poetry, concentrating on four of the greatest poets of the era: Friedrich Hölderlin, Johann Wolfgang von Goethe, Heinrich Heine and Novalis. Includes selections of their works at the back.

Samuel Beckett Goes Into the Silence
by Jeremy Mark Robinson

In the Dim Void: Samuel Beckett's Late Trilogy:
Company, Ill Seen, Ill Said and Worstward Ho
by Gregory Johns

Andre Gide: Fiction and Fervour in the Novels
by Jeremy Mark Robinson

The Ecstasies of John Cowper Powys
by A.P. Seabright

Amorous Life: John Cowper Powys and the Manifestation of Affectivity
by H.W. Fawkner

Postmodern Powys: New Essays on John Cowper Powys
by Joe Boulter

Rethinking Powys: Critical Essays on John Cowper Powys
edited by Jeremy Mark Robinson

Thomas Hardy and John Cowper Powys: Wessex Revisited
by Jeremy Mark Robinson

Thomas Hardy: The Tragic Novels
by Tom Spenser

Julia Kristeva: Art, Love, Melancholy, Philosophy, Semiotics
by Kelly Ives

Luce Irigaray: Lips, Kissing, and the Politics of Sexual Difference
by Kelly Ives

Helene Cixous I Love You: The Jouissance of Writing
by Kelly Ives

Emily Dickinson: *Selected Poems*
selected and introduced by Miriam Chalk

Petrarch, Dante and the Troubadours: The Religion of Love and Poetry
by Cassidy Hughes

Dante: *Selections From the Vita Nuova*
translated by Thomas Okey

Rainer Maria Rilke: *Selected Poems*
translated by Michael Hamburger

Walking In Cornwall
by Ursula Le Guin

GERMAN ROMANTIC POETRY

GERMAN ROMANTIC POETRY

Goethe, Novalis, Heine, Hölderlin

Carol Appleby

CRESCENT MOON

First published 1994. Second edition 2008. Fourth edition 2012.

Design by Radiance Graphics.
Printed and bound in the U.S.A.
Set in Book Antiqua 10 on 14pt.

British Library Cataloguing in Publication data

Appleby, Carol
German Romantic Poetry: Goethe, Novalis, Heine, Hölderlin.
– 3rd ed. (European Writers)
1. Goethe, Johann Wolfgang von, 1749-1832 – Criticism and Interpretation.
2. Novalis, 1772-1801 – Criticism and Interpretation.
3. Heine, Heinrich, 1797-1856 – Criticism and Interpretation.
4. Hölderlin, Friedrich, 1770-1843 – Criticism and Interpretation.
5. Romanticism.
I. Title
305.4201

ISBN-13 9781861713254 (Pbk)
ISBN-13 9781861713582 (Hbk)

Crescent Moon Publishing
P.O. Box 1312,
Maidstone, Kent,
ME14 5XU, Great Britain
www.crmoon.com

CONTENTS

❦

ACKNOWLEDGEMENTS

Anvil Press Poetry for permission to reprint from Michael Hamburger's translations in Friedrich Hölderlin, *Poems and Fragments*, Anvil Press Poetry, 1994.

Some of the translations of Friedrich Hölderlin are available from Crescent Moon, in *Hölderlin's Songs of Light: Selected Poems*. Novalis' *Hymns To the Night* and *Spiritual Songs* are also available from Crescent Moon.

Johann Wolfgang von Goethe

Heinrich Heine

Novalis

Friedrich Hölderlin

1

THE GERMAN ROMANTIC WORLD

The world must be romanticized.

Novalis, *Pollen and Fragments* (56)

Just as poetry is the most original, the arche–and mother–art of all the others, poetry will also be the ultimate perfection of humanity, the ocean into which however far it may have moved away from it in various forms.

A.W. Schlegel[1]

This book looks at German Romantic poetry chiefly in terms of its poetic, lyrical, magical, spiritual and erotic aspects. That is, poetry as poetry. The world of German Romantic poetry holds many of the same tenets as that of British or French Romanticism. We are not concerned here with definitions of the term 'Romanticism', which are discussed by critics elsewhere. Our definition of the term 'Romanticism' is of a lyrical, emotional, religious and self–conscious form of art which can be applied to many modern artists, as well as the Romantics themselves. 'Romanticism' is used

---

1 A.W. Schlegel, 1989–, I, 388

loosely, though applied mainly to the artists of the Romantic era, the late 18th and early 19th centuries. One can just as easily read Johann Wolfgang von Goethe, for instance, as a 'Classical' artist. Ditto Friedrich Schlegel, Novalis or Friedrich Hölderlin.[2] We are here studying the work of the poets, but not so much whether they were 'Classic' or 'Romantic', though connections will be made, from time to time, between Romanticism and modernism.[3]

The hallmarks of poetic Romanticism include the following:

Infinity.

'A work is shaped when it is everywhere sharply delimited, but within those limits limitless and inexhaustible; when it is completely faithful to itself, homogeneous, and nonetheless exalted above itself', wrote Karl Wilhelm Friedrich Schlegel in the *Athenaeum*.[4] The German Romantic poets, like the British and French writers, stretch themselves to infinity. If 'infinity' is an 'impossible' concept, scientifically, that does not bother the Romantics. They yearn towards infinity – in all things. As Percy Bysshe Shelley wrote in *A Defence of Poetry*, '[a] poet participates in the eternal, the infinite, and the one'.[5] Romanticism sometimes gives other names to its infinity–drive or extremism: the 'absolute' for instance, is frequently used: Romantics speak of absolute unity, absolute feeling, absolute art.

This extremism is a key component of Romanticism, whether it is the Romanticism of Johann Wolfgang von Goethe, Percy Shelley, Alfred de Musset or Novalis. Later artists, too, spoke of the necessity of 'going to extremes', such as André Gide, who wrote of extremism in his 1890s fiction, *Paludes*. Any number of

---

2 In German Romanticism, everyone is called 'Friedrich', or 'Wilhelm'.
3 See Jürgen Habermas: *The Philosophical Discourse of Modernity*, tr. Frederick Lawrence, MIT Press, Cambridge Mass., 1987. On German Romanticism, see David Simpson *et al*, eds: *German Aesthetic and Literary Criticism*, Cambridge University Press, 3 vols, 1984–5; H.G. Schenk: *The Mind of the European Romantics*, Constable 1966; M.H. Abrams, 1971; Manfred Brown, 1979; Philippe Lacoue–Labarthe, 1988; Azade Seyhan: *Representation and its Discontents: The Critical Legacy of German Romanticism*, University of California Press, Berkeley 1992
4 F. Schlegel: *Lucinde and the Fragments*, 297
5 P. Shelley: *Selected Poetry and Prose*, ed. Alisdair D.F. Macrae, Routledge 1991, 207

post–Romantic artists use the doctrine of extremism or going to infinity: William Burroughs with his outrageously violent novels, D.H. Lawrence with his wild flights of polemic, the painter Mark Rothko's canvases, everywhere regarded as 'Romantic', or Friedrich Nietzsche's philosophy.

Feeling.

Deep emotions, feelings or sensibilities are one of the most obvious marks of Romanticism. Romantic poetry goes mad with emotion, passion, elation. Romantic poetry can be reduced to one word: *desire*. It is all about desire, about the gulf between desire and satisfaction, between present desire and past fulfilment. As Heinrich Heine writes in *The Homecoming*:

> They both were in love, but neither
> To the other ever confessed;
> They acted so very unfriendly,
> And love burned high in each breast.[6]

Romantic poetry pivots around the Lacanian *lack*; the creation of Romantic poetry, as of nearly all poetry except that written to order, stems from some kind of desire. In Romantic poetry, the desire is for all manner of things – for love, connection, nature, infinity, ecstasy, etc. A.W. Schlegel speaks of the Romantic poetry of desire:

> The poetry of the ancients was the poetry of possession, our poetry is that of yearning; the former stands firmly on the ground of the present, the latter sways between memory and presentiment.[7]

Romantic poetry is fraught with all manner of tensions. One of the most fundamental is that between sacred and secular love. Love must be spiritualized, made transcendent, the Romantic poets contend. Or, as Friedrich Schlegel says, sacred and profane love must be harmonized. This form of spiritual love is, Schlegel

---

6 H. Heine: *Complete Poems*, 90
7 A.W. Schlegel: *Sämtliche Werke*, ed. Eduard Böcking, Weidmann, Leipzig 1846, 5,

writes: 'an intimation of the higher, the infinite, a hieroglyph of the one eternal love, of the sacred life-abundance of creative nature.'[8]

Ecstasy.

The apotheosis of feeling or desire in (German) Romantic poetry is ecstasy, just as in traditional religion. Ecstasy comes from all manner of input, ranging from nature contemplation through love and sex to drugs (the opiates, morphine or laudanum or whatever). Ecstasy is a goal of some (not all) Romantic poets. Novalis, John Keats and Friedrich Hölderlin were shamanic poets who at times whipped up storms of rapture. The sensual nature of Romantic poetry is obvious. At times, Romantic poetry is orgasmic, and the lush imagery, floods of words and shamanic energy combine to create an bliss of poetry, an erotic lyricism that is certainly one of the main reasons why Romantic poetry is so enjoyed by readers, and exalted by critics.

The Romantic poets burst life back into poetry, and their poetic personas (quite distinct from the poets as flesh and blood people, the subjects of biographies), burst into life themselves. So much of Romantic poetry is full of rapture, expressed in those single words – *life, love, soul, world* – energized by being written with capitals, accompanied by exclamation marks, so they become 'Life! Love! Soul! World!' Percy Bysshe Shelley's exuberant outburst is probably the most famous example of rapturous, exclamation marks Romanticism:

I

O world! O life! O time!
On whose last steps I climb,
   Trembling at that where I had stood before;
When will return the glory of your prime?
       No more – Oh, nevermore!

---

8 F. Schlegel, 1958–, II, 334

II

Out of the day and night
A joy has taken flight;
   Fresh spring, and summer, and winter hoar,
Move my faint heart with grief, but with delight
     No more – Oh, never more!

Mysticism.

Romantic poetry, and especially German Romantic poetry, is mystical. It is a religion on its own. It is a mystical cult, with its own initiations, rituals, beliefs, heresies and ecstasies. Friedrich Schlegel spoke of German Romantic poetry as something of a religion. Novalis and Schlegel referred to their attempt at founding a new religion.[9]

Novalis is the most obviously, flamboyantly mystical of the German Romantic poets, but Friedrich Hölderlin, Johann Wolfgang von Goethe and Heinrich Heine are no less mystical. That is, Novalis is unabashed about his mysticality: he leaps in, wholeheartedly.

Greece.

Romantic poets exalt Greek culture – Friedrich Hölderlin with his Hellenic hymns, for instance. A.W. Schlegel wrote that Greek culture was 'a perfect natural education', that Greek religion was the 'worship of natural forces and of earthly life', that the Greek concept of beauty was 'a purified, ennobled sensuality', that Greek art was a 'poetics of joy', the 'expression of the consciousness of this harmony of all forces'.[10]

All of the major German Romantic poets look back to Greece and, especially, to Greek mythology (but also back to the mediæval era, to the Renaissance, to poets such as William Shakespeare, Dante Alighieri and Giovanni Boccaccio, to the Orient, and to the early years of Christianity. The Schlegels studied Dante, Shakespeare, Boccaccio, Miguel de Cervantes,

---

9 See Ernst Behler, 158
10 A.W. Schlegel: *Sämtliche Werke*, op.cit., 5, 12–3

Francesco Petrarch, Calderón, Portuguese and Provençal poets).[11]

For the Romantics, the pantheon of Greek Gods and Goddesses were not simply reduced to words but fully alive beings, each with their own history, identity, personality and relationships.

Mythology/ Folklore.

A.W. Schlegel wrote: 'Myth, like language, general, a necessary product of the human poetic power, an arche-poetry of humanity'.[12] Much of German Romanticism uses all kinds of folklore – the Grimms, for instance, with their very influential collection and rewriting of fairy tales; Ludwig von Tieck's works contain much fantastic material, and he uses fairy tales in his fictions, including Charles Perrault's *Puss in Boots* fairy tale in his *Der gestiefelte Kater*;[13] Novalis wrote of fairy tales: 'All fairy tales are dreams of that homelike world that is everywhere and nowhere.'[14] Many poets looked back to Arthurian legends (John Keats in 'La Belle Dame Sans Merci', for instance); figures such as Isolde and Tristan, Tannhäuser, etc, appear in German Romantic poetry. Romanticism also employs all manner of 'hermetic' or 'occult' thought, from Gnosticism (in Novalis), Qabbalism, Rosicrucianism, alchemy, magic, astronomy, etc (in Franz Brentano's *Die Romanzen vom Rosenkrantz*, alchemy in Johann Wolfgang von Goethe's *Faust*, etc).

Paganism.

The Hellenism ties in (and is inextricable from) the paganism of Romanticism. The German Romantics, like their British counterparts, exalted pagan beliefs, though theirs was a stylized, self–conscious form of paganism, which took up certain beliefs or

---

11 See F. Schlegel, 1958, III, 17–37; E. Behler, 154; A.W. Schlegel: *Spanisches Theater*, Reimer, Berlin 1803–9, I, 2, 72–87
12 A.W. Schlegel, 1989-, I, 49
13 See Rolf Stamm: *Ludwig Tieck's späte Novellen*, Kohlhamer, Stuttgart 1973; Raimund Belgardt: "Poetic Imagination and External Reality in Tieck", *Essays in German Literature Festschrift*, ed. Michael S. Batts, University of British Columbia Press, 1968, 41–61; Rosemarie Helge: *Motive und Motivstrukturen bei Ludwig Tieck*, Kummerle, Göppingen 1974
14 Novalis: *Novalis Schriften*, 2, 564

rites and ignored others. Heinrich Heine wrote that the first Romantics

> acted out of a pantheistic impulse of which they themselves were not aware. The feeling which they believed to be a nostalgia for the Catholic Mother Church was of deeper origin than they guessed, and their reverence and preference for the heritage of the Middle Ages, for the popular beliefs, diabolism, magical practices, and witchcraft of that era… all this was a suddenly reawakened but unrecognized leaning toward the pantheism of the ancient Germans.[15]

The paganism of Romanticism is a part of pantheism, as in the Classicism of painters such as Nicolas Poussin and Claude Lorrain, or nature worship. Heinrich Heine called pantheism 'the secret religion of Germany'.[16]

Nature.

The Romantics exalted nature (German Romanticism had its 'Naturphilosophie', a non–scientific notion stemming partly from Friedrich Wilhelm Joseph Schelling and Georg Wilhelm Friedrich Hegel). But, again, nature is mediated through the highly self–conscious and heavily stylized mechanisms of poetry. Images of nature abound in most forms of Romantic poetry. Nature is the backdrop to their poetic out-pourings, but it is always nature seen from the vantage point of culture.

In *The Sorrows of Young Werther*, Johann Wolfgang von Goethe speaks of 'my heart's immense and ardent feeling for living Nature, which overwhelmed me with so great a joy and made the world about me a very paradise'. He goes on to evoke rivers and hilltops right out of European landscape painting, and 'lovely clouds which a soft evening breeze wafted across the heavens'.

> I felt as if I had been made a god in that overwhelming abundance, and the glorious forms of infinite Creation moved in my soul, giving it life. Immense mountains surrounded me, chasms yawned at my feet, streams swollen by rain tumbled headlong, rivers flowed below me

---

15 H. Heine: *Salon II*, 1852, 250–1
16 H. Heine: *Works*, 3, 571

and the forests and mountains resounded. (65)

Idealism

German Romantic poetry, like all Romantic poetry (like all poetry, one might say), has idealistic and utopian elements. German Romantic poetry, in particular, is marked by a vivacious, sometimes ridiculous idealism, which comes as much from Plato as from Immanuel Kant. 'Transcendental idealism' is a term often applied to German Romantic poetics. 'I call transcendental all knowledge which is not so much occupied with objects as with the mode of our cognition of objects', wrote Immanuel Kant in the *Critique of Pure Reason*,[17] underlining the subjectivity (as with René Descartes) that is at the centre of post–Renaissance philosophy. There is a philosophy, Johann Gottlieb Fichte argued, that is beyond being and beyond consciousness, a philosophy that aims for 'the absolute unity between their separateness.'[18]

Unity.

'The new mythology must be forged from the deepest depths of the spirit; it must be the most artful of all works of art, for it must encompass all others; a new bed and vessel for the ancient, eternal fountainhead of poetry', wrote Friedrich Schlegel.[19] One of the key elements of Romantic poetry, of German Romantic poetry especially, and of all poetry generally, is the concept of unity. For the poet, all things are connected together.

> In our mind [wrote Novalis], everything is connected in the most peculiar, pleasant, and lively manner. The strangest things come together by virtue of one space, one time, an odd similarity, an error, some accident. In this manner, curious unities and peculiar connections originate – one thing reminds us of everything, becomes the sign of many things. Reason and imagination are united through time and space in the most extraordinary manner, and we can say that each thought, each phenomenon of our mind is the most individual part of an

17 Immanuel Kant: *Werke*, de Gruyter, Berlin, 1968, III, 43
18 J. Fichte, letter, 23 June 1804, quoted in E. Behler, 19
19 F. Schlegel: *Dialogue on Poetry and Literary Aphorisms*, tr. Ernst Behler & Roman Struc, Pennsylvania State University Press, University Park 1968, 81–2

altogether individual totality.[20]

What connects it all is the poet's sensibility, awareness, imagination, talents, feelings, call them what you will. Poetry is very much like Western magic in this respect. Magicians speak of the cardinal rule of hermeticism and magicke as being the hermetic tenet of the Emerald Table of Hermes Trismegistus: *as above, so below*. This dictum applies to poetry as much to magic. Basically, the view is that all things are one even as they are separate/ different/ scattered everywhere. Sufi mystics speak of 'unity in multiplicity' and 'multiplicity in unity', the 'unity' for them being Allah. For poets and magicians, founded in the Western Neoplatonic, Renaissance, humanist, magical tradition, 'the One' is only occasionally identified with God.

For (the Romantic) poets, the *as above, so below* philosophy means that inner and outer are identical, that what happens inside, psychologically, is mirrored and influences the outer, physical world. The two worlds interconnect and influence each other. As Novalis writes: 'What is outside me, is really within me, is mind – and vice versa'.[21] Further, the world is a continuum for the poet, so that colours are associated with particular planets, say, or angels, or flowers, or metals. This view of the oneness of all things occurs not only in Romantic poetry, but in most of poetry, from Sappho onwards. It is, partly, the basis for the 'pathetic fallacy', the ubiquitous poetic metaphor, where Sappho can say that erotic desire is like a wind shaking oak trees on a mountainside.

The Romantic philosophy of unity develops into Charles Baudelaire's 'theory of correspondences', which was later taken up by Arthur Rimbaud, Stéphane Mallarmé and Paul Valéry. Friedrich Schlegel, one of the major theorists of Romantic poetry, speaks of Romantic poetry as unifying poetry and philosophy, which is one of the hallmarks of Romantic poetry, German or otherwise. 'Romantic poetry is a progressive universal poetry', wrote

20 Novalis: *Novalis Schriften*, 3, 650–1
21 Novalis: *Novalis Schriften*, 3, 429

Schlegel.[22] He argued for a new mythology of poetry, a universal mythopœia, which would connect all things together, a 'hieroglyphic expression of nature around us'.[23]

Ego / Subjectivity.

Since the Renaissance, 'the One' has been variously interpreted: a common interpretation is that all things relate, ultimately, to the human individual. Renaissance philosophy centres around the individual, where 'man is the measure of all things', embodied in Leonardo da Vinci's famous drawing *The Proportions of the Human Body*.[24] In the Renaissance view, man is at the centre of the universe. This is also very much the Romantic view. Catherine Belsey writes:

> One of the main thrusts of Romanticism is the rejection of an alien world of industrial capitalism, recurrently signified in images of death, disease and decay. Poetry claims to create a living world, fostered by nature but springing essentially from the subjectivity of the poet, from what Coleridge calls the Imagination, a mode of perception which endows the phenomenal world with a vitality and an intensity issuing ultimately from the soul itself... The Romantic rejection of the 'real conditions' is based on a belief in the autonomy of the subject. The 'man possessed of more than usual organic sensibility' greets in solitude the experiences he himself generates. But the escape, the transcendence, is rapidly seen to double back on itself: the higher knowledge proves to be a dream of a reversion to the very reality whose antithesis it was to represent.[25]

---

22 F. Schlegel, 1958, II, 182
23 F. Schlegel, in ib., II, 318
24 Leonardo: *The Proportions of the Human Body*, after Vitruvius, pen and ink, *c.* 1492, Accademia, Venice
25 Catherine Belsey: *Critical Practice*, Routledge 1980, 122

2

GOETHE

Goethe's philosophy is truly epic.

Novalis, *Pollen and Fragments*[26]

There is one great writer or poet in a country who, in the opinion of many critics, rises above all the other writers. William Shakespeare in Britain, Dante Alighieri in Italy, Homer in Greece, Leo Tolstoy in Russia, perhaps Victor Hugo in France, and, in Germany, Johann Wolfgang von Goethe. Goethe is the major poet of Germany. As Christopher Middleton writes: '[f]or two centuries Goethe has been the major figure in the history of German literature.'[27] Goethe is the 'last Renaissance man', according to Oswald Spengler. Certainly he wrote many different, but connected, kinds of work, from lyrics to natural science studies, from plays to memoirs. For Wolfgang Menzel, though, Goethe's art was apolitical, immoral and frivolous.[28]

---

26 Novalis: *Pollen and Fragments*, 40
27 C. Middleton, Introduction to Goethe: *Selected Poems*, xv. See also T.J. Reed: *The Classical Centre: Goethe and Weimar, 1775–1832*, Clarendon Press 1986
28 W. Menzel: *Die deutsche Litteratur*, Hallberger'sche Verlagshandlung, Stuttgart, 1836, III, 343

Johann Wolfgang von Goethe was born in Frankfurt on August 28, 1749, and died in Weimar on March 22, 1832. Goethe's key works include *Faust, Wilhelm Meister's Apprenticeship, The Sorrows of Young Werther, Iphigenie auf Tauris, Egmont, Torquato Tasso, Elective Affinities, Reineke Fuchs, Roman Elegies, The Natural Daughter, Theory of Colours* and *Venetian Epigrams*.

Here we look at some of Johann Wolfgang von Goethe's poems. It would take another volume and a half (at least) to deal with, say, the role of alchemy in *Faust*, or the relation of classicism to his philosophy. His is a mind full of ideas, not fully worked out into 'systems', but rich nevertheless.[29] His 'theory of colours', is fascinating (and influenced Britain's greatest painter, J.M.W. Turner, among others).

Ideas flow in Johann Wolfgang von Goethe's poetry, his poems resound with investigations in the fields of natural science, occult phenomena, Christian mysticism, philosophy, etc. He brings so much thought together in the crucible of his poems. One is reminded of Samuel Taylor Coleridge talking about how he would limber up for an epic poem:

> I should not think of devoting less than twenty years to an Epic Poem. Ten, to collect materials and warm my mind with universal science. I would be a tolerable mathematician. I would thoroughly know Mechanics, Hydrostatics, Optics, all Astronomy, Botany, Metallurgy, Fossilism, Chemistry, Geology, Anatomy, Medicine – then the *mind of man*, then the *minds of men* – in all Travels, Voyages and Histories.[30]

For Peter Redgrove, Johann Wolfgang von Goethe was a shamanic poet who was open to the 'streams' of the natural world. He is open to clairvoyance, occultism, the 'underside' of life, you might say. Redgrove writes:

---

29 See Gerhard Neumann: *Ideenparadiese: Untersuchungen zur Aphoristik von Lichtenberg, Novalis, Friedrich Schlegel und Goethe*, Fink, Munich 1976; Uwe Petersen: *Goethe und Euripdes*, Heidelberg, Winter 1974; Ronald Taylor, 1970; Ralph Tymms, 1955; Gerhard S. Kallienke: *Das Verhältnis von Goethe und Runge im Zusammenhang methes Auseinandersetzung mit der Frühr*, Buske, Hamburg 1973
30 S.T. Coleridge, letter to Joseph Cottle, Spring 1797, *Works*, Nonesuch 1933, 573

One can argue that Goethe was of, or was aware of, a masculine lineage distinct from that of Oedipus, a lineage represented by Tiresias, Faust, the English Merlin: the reborn magician in league with the 'dark' feminine powers, with the animals, possessing enlarged and clairvoyant senses. Goethe proceeded in his redemptive drama to show Faust after his bad start, in continued dialogue with the powers that he had called up. This is the non–Oedipal solution, to proceed in dialogue with your visions; the magical, or Romantic solution. All Romantics have followed it, or attempted to, even though it has led them to the darkest regions and to facing up to the hauntings created by Oedipal repression.[31]

There is much darkness in German Romantic (and most Romantic) poetry: big, windy moonlit skies such as, in later literature, fill Tom Brangwen's head in *The Rainbow* by D.H. Lawrence, or Arthur Rimbaud's soul in *A Season in Hell*, or, most obviously, that blow right through the work of Rainer Maria Rilke, ending up as the shamanic forces of the Angel in the *Duino Elegies*. These huge, cloudy, rainy, windy spaces are to be found not only in Johann Wolfgang von Goethe's poetry and his *Faust*, but also in Joseph Freiherr von Eichendorff's lyrics, in Heinrich Heine's *The North Sea* cycle, where the poet languishes on a nocturnal strand straight out of a Caspar David Friedrich painting, or in, of course, Novalis' *Hymnen an die Nacht*.

In Johann Wolfgang von Goethe's poetry, there is an impressive current of hermetic or occult thought, for Goethe is certainly a 'Renaissance man', a Renaissance mind.[32] There are many ideas in Goethe that come from the Renaissance – or, more accurately, from Neoplatonism as percolated through Renaissance philosophy. The identification, for instance, of inner and outer, so important to Occidental metaphysics. As Goethe writes in 'Epirrhema':

Müsset im Naturbetrachten,
Immer eins wie alles achten:

31 Peter Redgrove: *The Black Goddess*, Bloomsbury 1987, xxv–xxvi
32 See Robert Avens: *Imagination is Reality*, Spring Publications, Dallas, 1980. See also Raymond Immerwahr: "Friedrich Schlegel's Essay on Goethe's *Meister*", *Monatshefte*, xlix, 1957, 1–21

Nichts ist drinnen, nichts ist draußen:
Denn was innen, das ist außen.
So ergreifet ohne Säumnis
Helig öffentlich Geheimnis.

[You must, when contemplating nature,
Attend to this, in each and every feature:
There's enough outside and nought within,
For she is inside out and outside in.
Thus will you grasp, with no delay,
The holy secret, clear as day.][33]

The 'theory of correspondences' is such an important part of poetry, from Romanticism to the present. It enables Arthur Rimbaud to bring all manner of things into a poem, so that, in *Alchemy of the Word*, from *A Season in Hell*, he can write:

J'aimais les peintures idiotes, dessus de portes, décors, toiles de saltim-banques, enseignes, enluminures, populaires; la littérature démodée, latin d'église, livres érotiques sans orthographe, romans de nos aïeules, contes de fées, petits livres de l'enfance, opéras vieux, refrains niais, rhythmes naïfs.

[I liked idiot paintings, over doors, stage sets, backcloths for acrobats, signs, popular prints, old-fashioned literature, church latin, erotic books with misspellings, novels of our grandmothers, fairy tales, little children's books, old operas, foolish refrains, naive rhythms. (My translation)]

Everything can be included in a poem – a poem can be as open as that, if you wish. And this is what Johann Wolfgang von Goethe did, drawing together so many different subjects in his lyrics. There is many in the One, and the One is many, says Goethe. Sometimes, for the Romantics, the One may be 'God', or 'Love', as it was for the troubadours. But just as often it is 'Nature', sometimes personified as a Goddess, a Mother Earth figure, but also as an elemental power that blows through the poetry of Percy Bysshe Shelley, William Wordsworth, Novalis,

---

33 J. Goethe: 'Epirrhema', translated in *Selected Poems*, 158–9. Unless otherwise stated, all quotes from Goethe's poetry are from this edition.

Friedrich Hölderlin and Goethe. Nature, says, Goethe, is everything – but at the same time. As he writes in 'Allerdings' ('True Enough'):

Nature has neither core
Nor outer rind,
Being all things at once. (237)

At the extreme point, that is, when poetry becomes mysticism, the One and the All merge. 'Enter the All, make full the universe!' cries Johann Wolfgang von Goethe in 'Universal Soul' ('Weltseele', 167). This doctrine is given an intensely *lyrical* treatment in the German Romantics. We have found such beliefs before in culture – in the writings of Neoplatonic thinkers Plotinus, Porphyry, Iamblichus and Proclus, and in the exquisite, sinuous paintings of Sandro Botticelli – but with Goethe and Novalis and the German Romantics, the Neoplatonic doctrine of the One is given a luminous, limpid treatment. In Goethe's art, mysticism is celebrated in poems that astonish with their brilliance and deftness and quickness, that clarity and com-pression that is so difficult to capture in translation. 'Ein und Alles' ('One and All') is a typical example of one of Goethe's lucid philosophical poems:

Im Grenzenlosen sich zu finden,
Wird gern der einzelne verschwinden,
Da löst sich aller überdruß;
Statt heißen Wündschen, wildem Wollen,
Statt lästgem Fordern, strengem Sollen
Sich aufzugeben ist Genuß.

Weltseele, komm, uns zu durchringen!
Dann mit dem Weltgeist selbst zu ringen,
Wird unserer Kräfte Hochberuf.
Teilnehmend führen gte Geister,
Gelinde leitend höchste meister
Zu dem, der alles schafft und schuf.

Und umzuschafen ds Geschaffne,

Damit sichs nicht zun Starren waffne,
Wirkt ewiges, lebendiges Tun.
Und was nicht Sonnen, farbigen Erden
In keinem Falle darf es ruhn.

Es soll sich regen, schaffend handeln,
Erst sich gestalten, dann verwandeln;
Nur scheinbar stehts Momente still.
Das Ewige regt sich fort in alen;
Denn alles muß in Nichts zertfallen,
Wenn es im Sein beharren will.

[In boundlessness, itself discovering there,
The singular would gladly disappear,
Satiety is then absolved quite:
Ardent wishing, savage will abate,
Strict obligation, coping, ah, with Fate:
In self–abandon is delight.

Soul of the world, soak into us, descend,
Then with the very *Weltgeist* to contend
Our finest faculties contract;
Spirits benign will guide and sympathize,
Sublimest masters gently ways devise
To the perpetual Creative Act.

And with effect to make creation new,
It weaponed rigour soon enough undo,
Action eternal, vivid, rose;
And what was not, now wishes to unfold,
Become unsullied suns, a colour world;
No circumference permits repose.

It has to move, to be creating deed,
First make its form, then, changing it, proceed;
All stopping, short – illusion's twist.
For the Eternal onward moves in all,
And into nothing everything must fall,
If it in being would persist.] (240–3)

As a love poet, Johann Wolfgang von Goethe is an exuberant
writer, manifesting all the usual hallmarks of love poets
throughout history, from Sappho to Robert Graves: introspection,

melancholy, desire, eroticism, suffering, masochism, idealism and nostalgia. Goethe has written many fine lyrics which glorify love as the apotheosis of being alive – in his 'May Song' ('Mailied'), which sings of the energy of Spring with unashamed eroticism and fervour:

> The sun's in glory!…
> And every pleasure
> For girl, for boy!
> The sun–warm country
> Of joy on joy!
> O love! O lovely! my golden girl! (11)

This is an early lyric, but this Platonic fervour runs throughout Johann Wolfgang von Goethe's poems. Heinrich Heine has written, like so many other poets, of the eroticism of Spring – 'the magic month of May', Heine writes.[34] 'Testament' ('Vermächt') of 1829 speaks breathlessly of philosophical idealism, where nothing is lost, for 'all' lives in the 'All':

> No thing on earth to nought can fall,
> The Eternal onward moves in all;
> Rejoice, by being be sustained.
> Being is deathless: living wealth,
> With which the all adorns itself,
> By laws abides and is maintained. (267)

In 'Night Thought' ('Nachtgedanken'), Johann Wolfgang von Goethe expresses the Renaissance belief in the primacy of humanity above other things, such as nature. Nature, Geothe says, or more particularly, stars, do not love: '[s]tars, you are unfortunate, I pity you… Love you do not, nor do you know what love is.' (83) Goethe's verse is very erotic and sensual, as erotic and sensual as any of the Romantics – John Keats at his richest, or Heinrich Heine, or Alfred de Musset. There are obvious moments of passion and sensuality in poems such as 'Elegie':

---

34 H. Heine: *Complete Poems*, 52

Der Kuß, der letzte, grausam süß, zerschneidend
Ein herriches Geflecht verschlungner Minnen.
Nun eilt, nun stockt der Fuß, die Schwelle meidend,
Als trieb' ein Cherub flammend ihn von hinnen;
Das Auge starrt auf düstrem Pfad verdrossen,
Es blickt zurück, die Pforte steht verschlossen.

Our final kiss, so shuddering sweet, it tore
The sheerest of All fibre, heart's desire.
My foot, abrupt or dragging, dodged her door
As if an angel waved that sword of fire.
Eyes frozen on the dusky ruts go glum.
Turn, and her door's a darkness, shut and dumb. (247)

Or this more fleshly extract from 'Roman Elegies' ('Romische elegien'):

Your plain woollen dress in a jiffy,
Unfastened by me, slips down, lies in its folds on the floor,
Quickly I carry the child in her flimsy wrapping of linen
As befits a good nurse, teasingly, into her bed.
Spacious for two, it stands free in a spacious room.
Then let Jupiter get more joy from his Juno, a mortal
Anywhere in this world know more contentment than I.
We enjoy the delights of the genuine naked god, Amor,
And our rock–a–bye bed's rhythmic, melodious creak. (105)

Like contemporary pop singers, like most love poets, Johann Wolfgang von Goethe, will try to find twenty thousand different ways of saying *I want you here now*. Or, as pop songs put: *I want to touch you*. 'How her figure haunts me! Waking or dreaming, she fills my entire soul!' cries the narrator of *The Sorrows of Young Werther*.

Johann Wolfgang von Goethe, in his love poet mode, will mouth banalities, using the time–worn metaphors of love poetry, as in this from 'The Bride of Corinth':

Breathless kiss on kiss!
Overflowing kiss!
"Dost thou burn and feel my burning fire?"

Closer still they cling and closer, mixing
Tears and cries of love, limbs interlaced,
She sucks his kisses, his with hers transfixing,
Each self aware the other it possessed. (139)

Johann Wolfgang von Goethe's eroticism will slip without any problems from 'realist', erotic excursions, to wistful, idealized laments on lost love, such as this poem 'Nearness of the Beloved', which mixes the usual natural mysticism of love poetry with erotic desire:

Ich denke dein, wenn mir der Sonne Schimmer
    Vom meere straht;
Ich denke dein, wenn sich des Mondes Flimmer
    In Quellen malt.

Ich sehe dich, wenn auf dem fernen Wege
    Der straub sich herbt;
In tiefer nacht, wenn auf dem schmalen Stege
    Der Wandrer bebt.

Ich höre dich, wenn dort mit dumpfen Rauschen
    Die Welle steigt.
Im stillen Haine geh ich oft zu lauschen,
    Wenn alles schweigt.

Ich bin bet dir, du seist auch noch so ferne,
    Du bist mir nah!
Die Sonne sinkt, bald leuchten mir die Sterne.
    O wärst du da!

[I think of you when from the sea the shimmer
    Of sunlight streams;
I think of you when on the brook the dimmer
    Moon casts her beams.

I see your face when on the distant highway
    Dust whirls and flakes,
In deepest night when on the mountain byway
    The traveller quakes.

I hear your voice when, dully roaring, yonder
    Waves rise and spill;

Listening, in silent woods I often wander
When all is still.

I walk with you, though miles from you divide me;
Yet you are near!
The sun goes down, soon stars will shine to guide me.
Would you were here!]. (128–9)

Johann Wolfgang von Goethe, like John Keats, Percy Bysshe
Shelley, Heinrich Heine or Novalis, is 'sore with bliss' when he's
in love (phrase from 'Submerged'/ 'Versunken', 209). He is the
poet who quests the Holy Grail of true love '[t]hrough labyrinths
of passion', as he puts it in 'Trilogy of Passion', very much in the
style of his novel *The Sorrows of Young Werther* (245).

In poems such as 'Presence' ('Gegenwart'), Johann Wolfgang
von Goethe evokes a fragile, yearning and transcendent form of
loving. 'Presence' is a Rilkean love poem a hundred years before
Rainer Maria Rilke, with its evocations of rose gardens, flowers,
moon and stars, eternity, glory and movement:

Alles kündet dich an!
Erscheinet die herrliche Sonne,
Folgst du, so hoff ich es, bald.

Trittst du im Garten hervor,
So bist du die Rose der Rosen,
Lilie der Lilien zugleich.

Wenn du im Tanze dich regst,
So regen sich alle Gestirne
mit dir und im dich umher.

Nach! und so wär es denn Nacht!
Nun überscheinst du des Mondes
Lieblichen, ladenden Glanz.

Ladend und lieblich bist du,
Und Blumen, Mond und Gestirne
Huldigen, Sonne, nur dir.

Sonne! so sei du auch mir

Die Schöpferin herrlicher Tage;
Leben und Ewigkeit ist.

[All's a foretelling of you.
Sun in its glory ascending,
Soon you will follow, I hope.

Into the garden you walk,
Rose of the roses you are,
Lily of lilies as well.

When you but move in the dance,
All of the stars are in motion
With you and round where you move.

Night! just let the night come!
Now you outshine the attractive
Delicate glow of the moon.

Delicate, fetching you are,
Flowers, the moon, and the stars
Celebrate, sun, only you.

Sun! be such to me too,
Creator of days in a glory;
Life and eternity – thus.] (194–5)

Johann Wolfgang von Goethe's poetry encompasses all aspects of Romantic poetry, from the purely lyrical, to the erotic, to the philosophical, to social commentary. Like all the Romantics, his poesie is very 'visual'; that is, it involves itself in conjuring up visions. There are many correlations between poetry in painting through the Romantic era. Goethe explores the correspondences in his 'Amor as a Landscape Painter' ('Amor als Landschaftsmaler'), where the creation of the poetic world of painting is compared to the creation of the emotional world of the lover:

Und er richtete den Zeigefinger,
Der so rötlich war wie eine Rose,
Nach dem weiten ausgespannten Tepich,
Fing mit seinem finger an zu zeichnen.

Oben malt' er eine schöne Sonne,
Die mir in die Augen mächtig glänzte,
Und den Saum Der Wolken macht' er golden,
Ließ die Strahlen durch die Wolken dringen;
Malte dann die zarten leichten Wipfel
Frisch erquickter Bäume, zog die Hügel,
Einen nach dem andern, frei dahinter;
Unten ließ ers nicht an Wasser fehlen,
Zeichnete den Fluß so ganz natürlich,
Daß er schien im sonnenstrahl zu glitzern,
Daß er schien am hohen Rand zu rauschen.

[Then he lifted up his index finger,
Which was quite as rosy as a rose is;
Pointing to the fabric stretched before him,
Now the boy began to trace a picture.

At the top a beauteous sun he painted,
I was almost blinded by the dazzle;
Borders of the clouds, he made them golden,
Rays of sun to perforate the cloud mass;
Painted then the delicate and tender
Tops of freshly quickened trees, with hillocks
Touched into place and freely grouped behind them;
Lower down – water he put, and plenty,
Drew the river, as it is in nature,
So much so, it seemed to glint with sunlight
And murmur as it rose against its edges.] (98–99)

Claude Lorrain is perhaps the painter or visualizer of Johann Wolfgang von Goethe's mythical landscapes. Claude's paintings of dreamy, blue–hazed Arcadias are the equivalent of Goethe's poetic visions (and especially in poems such as 'Amor as Landscape Painter'). In Goethe, vision veers from that of natural science (as in 'The Metamorphosis of Plants', with its marvellous evocations of delicate, unfurling plants entwining with each other), to Dantean visions of mystical illumination and wonder. In 'Dedication' the narrator is dazzled by a Beatrice or *anima* figure – in short, a Goddess:

Then in the glory–cloud that seemed to bear her

A godlike woman drifted through the air;
I never did behold a vision fairer,
And now she gazed upon me, floating there. (91)

The vision of the Goddess appears again in 'Wanderer's Storm-Song' ('Wanderers Sturmlied'), of 1772, where the poet invokes the Graces and Muses:

You are pure, like water's heart,
You are pure, like earth's marrow,
Round me you float and I
Float over water, over earth,
Godlike. (19)

What Johann Wolfgang von Goethe inaugurates in German poetry is a particular kind of lyrical poetry that forms the basis, in a sense, of all that comes after him: Novalis through to Rainer Maria Rilke and beyond. It is a certain kind of radiant lyricism that pulls together philosophy, love poetry, religion and nature poetry, a poetry which you might call 'transcendent poetry', which became the major factor in Rilke's poetry. Goethe's 'transcendent poetry' is found in short lyrics such as 'To the Full Moon Rising', where the poet writes of the 'rapturous night' (263), or the equally ethereal 'Twilight down from Heaven', which, as the title suggests, sees twilight as descending from heaven with a lustre, a beauty and a coolness that calms the narrator's heart (261). Poems such as 'Permanence in Change' ('Dauer im Wechsel'), quoted here in full, are pure Goethe, and Goethe at his best, drawing together eroticism, philosophy, nature mysticism, the seasons, time and insight in a deceptively simple lyrical form:

Hielte diesen frühen segen
Ach, nur Eine Stunde fest!
Aber vollen Blütenregen
Schüttelt schon der laue West.
Soll ich much des Grünen freuen,
Dem ich Schatten erst verdankt?
Bald wird Sturm auch das zersteuen,

Wenn es falb im Herbst geschwankt.

Willst du nach den Früchten greifen,
Eilig nimm dein Teil davon!
Diese fangen an zu reifen,
Und die andern keimen schon;
Gleich mit jedem Regengusse
Andert sich dein holdes Tal,
Ach, und in demselben Flusse
Schwimmst du nicht zum zweitenmal.

Du nun selbst! Was felsenfeste
Such vor dir hervorgetan,
Mauern siehst du, siehst Paläste
Stets mit andern Augen an.
Weggeschwunden ist die Lippe,
Die im Kusse sonst genas,
Jener Fuß, der an der Klippe
Sich mit Gemsenfreche maß.

Jene Hand, die gern und milde
Sich bewigte wohzutun,
Das gegliederte Gebilde,
Alles ist ein andres nun.
Und was sich an jener Stele
Nun mit deinem Namen nent,
Kam herbei wie eine Welle,
Und so eilts zum Element.

Laß den Anfang mit dem Ende
Sich in Eins zusammenziehn!
Schneller als die Gegenstände
Selber dich vorüberfliehn.
Danke, daß die Gunst der Musen
Unvergängliches verheißt,
Den Gerhalt in deinem busen
Und die form in deinem Geist.

[Early blossoms – could a single
Hour preserve them just as now!
But the warmer west will scatter
Petals showering from the bough.
How to enjoy these leaves, that lately
I was grateful to for shade?

Soon the wind and snow are rolling
What the late Novembers fade.

Fruit – you'd reach a hand and have it?
Better have it then with speed.
These you see about to ripen,
Those already gone to seed.
Half a rainy day, and there's your
Pleasant valley not the same,
None could swim that very river
Twice, so quick the changes came.

You yourself! What all around you
Strong as stonework used to be
– Castles, battlements – you see them
With an ever–changing eye.
Now the lips are dim and withered
Once the kisses set aglow;
Lame the leg, that on the mountain
Left the mountain goat below.

Or that hand, that knew such loving
Ways, outstretching in caress,
– Cunningly adjusted structured–
Now can function less and less.
All are gone; this substitution
Has your name and nothing more.
Like a wave it lifts and passes,
Back to atoms on the shore.

See in each beginning, ending,
Double aspects of the One;
Her, amid stampeding objects,
Be among the first to run,
Thankful to a nurse whose favour
Grants you one unchanging thing:
What the heart can hold to ponder;
What the spirit shape to sing.] (168-9)

It is these exquisite and delicate moments of pure lyricism that
makes Johann Wolfgang von Goethe and the German Romantics
so distinctive. For they align this experience of
being–in–the–world, this nature mysticism some would call it,

with the central facts of being alive. Thus, the experience of twilight in Goethe, which Oswald Spengler noted in *The Decline of the West*, is, for Goethe and the Romantics, a central experience, not something decentred, marginalized, on the outside. Goethe's poetry, though immensely cultured, learned, 'civilized', is not based on an urban experience, but one of the country. However, it is always nature as mediated by people. At the centre of the Goethean mythopœic experience is the human being, not nature. It is man, Goethe believes, who draws everything together, in Renaissance fashion, who is the measure of all things. This view is the modern one, with its emphasis on subjectivity and individual response. As Goethe writes in his 'The Godlike' ('Das Göttliche'):

man alone can
Achieve the impossible:
He distinguishes,
Chooses and judges;
He can give lasting
Life to the moment... (81)

3

HÖLDERLIN

Friedrich Hölderlin's life was remarkable, and is worth looking at in some detail: he was born Johann Friedrich Hölderlin on March 20, 1770 in Lauffen, a Swabian town on the River Neckar. Much has been made of his relationship with his mother, and his dependence on her (his father died in 1772, when Hölderlin was an infant, and his step-father died in 1779). Hölderlin studied at the local grammar school until 1784; he was a boarder at the Lower Monastery School (in Denkendorf) and the Upper Monastery School (in Maulbronn). At Tübingen, a town that crops up many times in Hölderlin's biography, he studied for his inordination from 1788-93. He wrote many poems at Tübingen, as well as student theses on the links between Solomon's proverbs and Hesiod's *Works and Days*, and on Greek art (*Die Geschichte der schönen Künste unter den Griechen*).

Since he was young Friedrich Hölderlin had worshipped Johann Christoph Friedrich von Schiller (1759-1805), so when he met him at Jena, Hölderlin was over-awed. The adoration seemed to be one-sided, Schiller regarding Hölderlin as an eager, talented but 'rather helpless young fellow-Swabian'. The friendship with

Schiller was crucial for Hölderlin. At times, in Jena, Hölderlin was so taken over by Schiller's presence that he was hardly aware of other people in the room – even luminaries such as Johann Wolfgang von Goethe, the king of German literature. Goethe did not or would not acknowledge Hölderlin's talent (Goethe also failed to recognize Heinrich Heine's creativity).

Friedrich Hölderlin did not take up the religious calling, the ministry, which his family (particularly his mother) had been expecting of him for years. Instead, Hölderlin became a private tutor. Working for Charlotte von Kalb's son, at Waltershausen, Hölderlin wrote his novel *Hyperion* in 1793. After his time with Frau von Kalb, Hölderlin spoke of wanting to live by writing alone, 'to keep my body and my soul alive by my own works' (in A. Stansfield, 41), one of the primary desires of all writers. His patron and mentor in the 1790s was Friedrich Schiller.

The chief love in Friedrich Hölderlin's life was Susette Gontard, the 'beautiful, cultured and noble' wife of a Frankfurt banker.[35] Hölderlin taught Gontard's children. Just as Novalis worshipped his beloved Sophie von Kühn as an embodiment of Sophia (Wisdom), a Goddess of transcendent philosophy, so Hölderlin apostrophized Susette Gontard as Diotima in poems such as 'Diotima', 'To Diotima', 'To Her Genius' and 'Menon's Lament for Diotima'. Diotima was the hero's beloved in Hölderlin's novel *Hyperion*.

It was with his relationship with Susette Gontard that Friedrich Hölderlin's poetry began to develop rapidly, achieving a depth and lyricism far beyond the early poems. Gontard, as Diotima, was crucial in this poetic development. Hölderlin's relationship with Gontard was relatively brief, however. They perhaps enjoyed a greater intimacy in 1796, when Gontard and her children evacuated Frankfurt for Kassel to avoid the French army. In 1798, though, Gontard sent Hölderlin away after an altercation, or he left secretly, depending on which biography is consulted.

Friedrich Hölderlin felt increasingly lonely from 1799 onwards,

---

35 L. Salzberger, 1952, 25.

a societal outsider. He was frustrated in finding a way of being a self-sufficient writer, and piquantly felt the separation from his lover, Gontard. The contacts with the greats of German Romant-icism (Goethe, Schiller, Novalis, Hegel) did not satisfy his ambitions.

It was after the return journey from Bordeaux that Friedrich Hölderlin suffered his 'madness'. Gontard was ill – she died on June 22, 1802, from German measles caught from her children. The news of her death, communicated to him by a letter to Christian Landauer from Isaak von Sinclair, one of Hölderlin's most devoted friends (written on June 30, 1802), may have contributed to his psychic decline. Certainly her death was a massive loss – she was his Muse, after all, and he valued poetry above nearly everything.

In August, 1806 Friedirch Hölderlin, after bouts of nervous exhaustion and colic, could no longer stay at Homburg. Hölderlin was taken by force to Autenrieth mental clinic in Tübingen. Here the regime included immersion in cold water in a cage, strait jackets, drugs (belladonna, digitalis), and the Autenrieth mask, put on to stop patients screaming.

Friedrich Hölderlin was rescued from this hell in the mental home by Ernst Zimmer, a carpenter, who took Hölderlin in 1807 to his house in Tübingen beside the River Neckar. Here, in a small room in Zimmer's 'tower', Hölderlin spent the rest of life (36 years), until his death on June 7, 1843, aged 73. Hölderlin's biography contains a huge gap of years, about which little is known.

Ernst Zimmer reckoned that Friedrich Hölderlin had 'too much in him' and it 'cracked his mind'. Certainly, from even a cursory glance at his biography, Hölderlin comes across as a determined and yearning soul. The failure of the magazine project due to lack of interest is disheartening, but is a sign of a general trend in Hölderlin's life where he felt distanced from society and social contact. The separation from Susette Gontard is more serious: here Hölderlin's feelings of ineffectuality must have been greater, for he could not lay claim to Gontard. He was always the outsider in the Gontard household, where his employer was master.

Ernst Meister wonders if Friedrich Hölderlin let himself become mad, to make up for the 'ordinary' life that everyday people lead, 'the provincial or parochial life, as it were, in the island's interior, against which the whole being surges and breaks' (1989). E.M. Butler reckons that Hölderlin's instability arose from having to choose between his beloved Greek gods and Christ. Hölderlin's decline into mental illness is disturbing to contemplate. Butler speaks of 'this gruesome wreck of one of the greatest poets in the world' (238).

In a letter to Ulrich Boehlendorff of December, 1802, Friedrich Hölderlin wrote 'as it has been said of heroes, I may say that Apollo has struck me'.[36] Some critics interpreted the line 'Apollo has struck me' as indicating sunstroke. The phrase expresses much of Hölderlin's outlook: the violence of the image is typical of Hölderlin's extreme emotions. He does not say 'melted softly in me', but 'struck me'. It is not the deity that is important – it might be Apollo, Zeus, Dionysius or Christ – but the force of the mystical influence. There is a feeling in Hölderlin's poetry that he is 'driven', and usually a sense, as with Friedrich Nietzsche, that he is being driven by a god (or the gods).

Friedrich Hölderlin believed in the notion of the poet as shaman, a *vates*, a prophet.[37] As he wrote in 'An die Deutschen' ('To the Germans'), 'sweet it is to divine, but an affliction too'[38] And he believed in his poetic world, as poets have to: 'Hölderlin's world was one in which he alone believed', wrote Alessandro Pelegrini.[39] His poetry is marked by a movement towards bliss, the ecstasy of the shaman, which Hölderlin does not suppress. Rather, he cultivates it scrupulously. His lyrics are pure lyrics, set in the Orphic mode, that way of making poetry that comes from Orpheus, the ancient deity of shamanic poetry. Mircea Eliade

---

36 In L. Salzberger, 39-40.
37 See L.S. Salzberger, 8–12
38 F. Hölderlin: *Poems and Fragments*, 123
39 Alessandro Pelegrini: *Hölderlin: Storia della Critica*, 1965, 414–5

writes thus of Orpheus and shamanism:

> As to Orpheus, his myth displays several elements that can be
> compared to the shamanic ideology and technique. The most significant
> is, of course, his descent to Hades to bring back the soul of his wife,
> Eurydice... Orpheus displays other characteristics of a "Great
> Shaman": his healing art, his love for music and animals, his "charms",
> his power of divination. Even his character of "culture hero" is not
> contradiction to the best shamanic tradition – was not the "first
> shaman" the messenger sent by God to defend humanity against
> diseases and to civilize it? A final detail of the Orpheus myth is clearly
> shamanic. Cut off by the bacchantes and thrown into the Gebrus,
> Orpheus' head floated to Lesbos, singing. It later served as an oracle...[40]

Friedrich Hölderlin's poetry, especially his early lyrics, is
powerfully shamanic; it is full of shamanic imagery, as is the
early poetry of Percy Shelley or Francesco Petrarch. In Hölderlin's
poetry we find images of light, of bliss, of motion, of revelation,
all shamanic/ religious motifs. Heinrich Heine's view of the poet
as shaman was more political, aware of the role of the poet in
societal revolutions:

> Our age is warmed by the idea of human equality, and the poets, who
> as high priests do homage to this divine sun, can be certain that
> thousands kneel down beside them, and that thousands weep and
> rejoice with them.[41]

'Hyperion's Song of Fate' is one of the best examples of
Friedrich Hölderlin's lyricism, his Orphic/ shamanic voice, his
Hellenism, and his triumphant use of the hymn or ode form:

> Ihr wandelt droben im Licht
>   Auf weichen Boden, seelige Genien!
>   Glänzende Götterlüfte
>   Rühren euch leicht,
>   Wie die Finger der Künstlerin
>   Heilige Saiten.

Schiksaallos, wie der schlafende

---

40 Mircea Eliade: *Shamanism*, 1972, 391
41 H. Heine: *The Works of Heinrich Heine*, tr. C.G. Leland *et al*, Heinemann, I, 432

Säugling, athmen die Himmlischen;
  Keusch bewahrt
    In bescheidener Knospe,
      Blühet ewig
        Ihnen der Geist,
          Und die seeligen Augen
            Bliken in stiller
              Ewiger Klarheit.

Doch uns ist gegeben,
  Auf keiner Stätte zu ruhn,
    Es schwinden, es fallen
      Die leidenden Menschen
        Blindlings von einer
          Stunde zur andern,
            Wie Wasser von Lippe
              Zu Lippe geworfen,
                Jahr lang ins Ungewisse hinab.

[You walk above in the light,
  Weightless tread a soft floor, blessed genii!
    Radiant the gods' mild breezes
      Gently play on you
        As the girl artist's fingers
          On holy strings.

Fateless the Heavenly breathe
  Like an unweaned infant asleep;
    Chastely preserved
      In modest bud
        For ever their minds
          Are in flower
            And their blissful eyes
              Eternally tranquil gaze,
                Eternally clear.

But we are fated
  To find no foothold, no rest,
    And suffering mortals
      Dwindle and fall
        Headlong from one
          Hour to the next,
            Hurled like water
              From ledge to ledge

Downward for years to the vague abyss.][41]

There are images of skies on fire at sunset in Friedrich Hölder-lin's poetry, archetypal images of Romantic poetry these, as in 'Abendphantasie' ('Evening Fantasy'), where the poet writes:

A springtime buds high up in the evening sky,
   There countless roses bloom, and the golden world
Seems calm, fulfilled; O there now take me,
   Crimson-edged clouds, and up there at last let

My love and sorrow melt into light and air! (91)

Out it all pours, pure feeling, expressed in concise, compressed stanzas, short lyrics which veer between free verse and highly formal poetry (Friedrich Hölderlin's hymns were based on the Pindaric ode), a poetry, like all ecstatic poetry, which threatens to break out of its formal boundaries and spill over in endless sentences and phrases, repeated, time after time. Hölderlin pours out his poetry with, at times, a seeming lack of self-conscious-ness. His lyrics seem to be expressions of feeling and nothing else, yet, at the same time, they are carefully controlled. There is a mystery, too, at the heart of Hölderlin's poetry, in the gaps between his words. Edwin Muir wrote:

> This omission of connecting links is characteristic of the poem, and I think of the kind of poetry to which it belongs, where mystery is not a thing to be explained, but a constant and permitted presence.[42]

In 'In the Morning' ('Des Morgens'), Friedrich Hölderlin sends out passionate lines to the sky, evocative incantations that poets have written or spoken since time immemorial:

Vom Thaue glänzt der Rasen; beweglicher
   Eilt schon die wache Quelle; die Buche neigt
      Ihr schwankes Haupt und im Geblätter

---

42 Edwin Muir: "Hölderlin's *Patmos*", in *The European Quarterly*, vol. 1, no.4, February, 1935

Rauscht es und schimmert; und um die grauen

Gewölke streifen röthliche flammen dort,
 Verkündende, sie wallen geräuschlos auf;
  Wie Fluthen am Gestade, woogen
   Höher und höher die Wandelbaren.

Komm nun, o komm, unde eile mir nicht zu schnell,
 Du goldner Tag, zum Gipfel des immels fort!
  Denn offner fliegt, vertrauter dir mein
   Aug, du Freudiger! zu, so lang du

In deiner Schöne jugendlich blikst und noch
 Zu herrlich nicht, zu stolz mor geworden bist;
  Do möchtest immer eilen, könnt ich,
   Göttlicher Wandrer, mit dir!

Des frohen übermüthigen du, daß er
 Dir gleichen möchte; seegne mir lieber dann
  Mein sterblich Thun und heitre wieder
   Gütiger! heute den stillen Pfad mir.

[With dew the lawn is glistening; more nimbly now,
 Awake, the stream speeds onward; the beech inclines
  Her limber head and in the leaves a
   Rustle, a glitter begins; and round the

Grey cloud-banks there a flicker of reddish flames,
 Prophetic ones, flares up and in silence plays;
  Like breakers by the shore they billow
   Higher and higher, the ever-changing.

Now come, O come, and not too impatiently,
 You golden day, speed on to the peaks of heavens!
  For more familiar and more open,
   Glad one, my vision flies up towards you

While youthful in your beauty you gaze and have
 Not grown too glorious, dazzling and proud for me;
  Speed as you will, I'd say, if only
   I could go with you, divinely ranging!

But at my happy arrogance now you smile,
 That would be like you; rather, then, rambler, bless

My mortal acts, and this day also,
    Kindly one, brighten my quiet pathway.] (93)

Like Johann Wolfgang von Goethe, Friedrich Hölderlin's philo-
sophy is founded on a mythical unity, where dualism is trans-
cended by the 'One and All' of ancient philosophy, the primal
unity of pantheism. Hölderlin's is a 'religion of the heart', a
pantheism in tune with his mythical heroes – above all,
Empodecles.[43] Hölderlin's poetry, like that of, say, William
Shakespeare, Sappho or Emily Dickinson, draws so many things
together. The poem becomes an alchemical vessel in which artistic
transformations occur. The poem becomes a Holy Grail or magical
cauldron in which poetic creations are fermented. 'My Possessions'
('Mein Eigentum'), for example, is a poem that brings together a
host of images and motifs and experiences, melded by the poet's
vision, his imagination, his poetics, his voice, his word magic. He
brings together in a magic mix the 'mellow grapes', 'red
orchards', Autumn, fields, crops, labour, heaven, light, corn,
gold, the breeze, joy, a rose, the homeland, and so on (98–101).

At times, Friedrich Hölderlin is more Rilkean than Rainer
Maria Rilke, more like Novalis than Novalis himself. Certainly
Hölderlin is part of this Germanic lyrical tradition, which stretches
from Angelus Silesius through the Romantics and Friedrich
Nietzsche, to Rilke and Georg Trakl. It is a tradition of lyrical
poetry that encompasses a poignant, soulful mysticism with a
generous nature love. It's a tradition founded on Christian
metaphysics and monastic/ mediæval mysticism which allows a
poetic expansion into the realms of supra–Christian/ pantheistic
thought. In 'Love' ('Die Liebe'), Hölderlin expresses sentiments
familiar to us from Rilke's *Sonnets to Orpheus*, where Rilke
implores us to become more than we are. Hölderlin apostrophizes
'Love', love as a God, the abstraction that was made into a deity
by the Greeks, so that the troubadours, a millennium later, could

---

43 See Arthur Häny: *Hölderlin's Titanenmythos*, Zurich 1948, Hermann Boesch-
enstein: *Deutsche Gefühlskultur*, Berne 1954, Michael Hamburger, *Reason And Energy*,
14f, Martin Heidegger: *Erläuterungen zu Hölderlin Dichtung*, Frankfurt, 1951

write endless *cansos* and lovesongs addressed to 'Love', or 'Eros', or 'Cupid'. In Hölderlin's mythopœia, 'Love' is not the 'Amor' of courtly love, but the God of pantheism, the spirit of life itself, which, as with Rilke, the poet implores to grow and grow:

Sei geseegnet, o sei, himmlische Pflanze, mir
   Mit Gesange gepflegt, wenn des ätherischen
      Nektars Kräfte dich nähren,
         Und der schöpfrische Stral dich reift.

Wachs und werde zum Wald! eine beseeltere,
   Vollentblühende Welt! Sprache der Liebenden
      Sei die Sprache des Landes,
         Ihre Seele der Laut des Volks!

[You, then, heavenly plant, now let me bless, and be
   Ever tended with song, when the ætherial
      Nectar's energies feed you,
         Ripened by the creative ray.

Grow and be a whole wood! be a more soul–inspired,
   Fully blossoming world! Language of lovers now
      Be the language our land speaks,
         And their soul be the people's lilt!] (145–7)

In the work of Friedrich Hölderlin, as with that of John Keats, Percy Bysshe Shelley, Novalis, Johann Wolfgang von Goethe, and other Romantic poets, personifications or abstractions such as 'Love', 'God', 'Life' and 'Nature' merge into one another. So that, in prating passionately of 'Love', the European poet may also be speaking of 'God'. But, just as easily, the poet may be speaking of 'Nature'. The object of the poet's incantation is less important than the incantation itself, the style and form and velocity and beauty of the incantation, the poem, itself. Thus, in the courtly love era, it was essential to carve a beautiful poem. It was part of the poet's form of loving that the poem itself should be a beautiful object. An ugly or roughly–hewn poem meant an ugly or a roughly–hewn love. The greater the refinement and sophistication of the *canso*, the greater the love of the poet. So too with William

Shakespeare, or C.P. Cavafy, or Hölderlin. The poem itself must be well–crafted.

Nature, Love, God, Life, World, they all fuse. So in one of his shamanic texts, where he sets out the poetics of the poet, Friedrich Hölderlin writes passionately of nature:

Und dennoch, o ihr Himmlischen all, und all
   Ihr Quellen und ihr Ufer und Hain' und Höhn,
      Wo wunderbar zuerst, als du die
         Loken ergriffen, und unvergeßlich

Der unverhoffte Genius über uns
   Der schöpferische, göttliche kam, daß stumm
      Der Sinn uns ward und, wie vom
         Strale gerührt das Gebein erbebte,

Ihr ruhelosen Thaten in weiter Welt!
[And yet, you heavenly powers, you all, and all
   You fountains, all you banks and you groves and peaks
      Where marvellous at first when by the
         Forelock you seized us, and unforeseen the

Divine, creative Genius came over us,
   Dumbfounding mind and sense, unforgettably,
      And left us as though struck by lightning
         Down to our bones that were still aquiver,

You restless deeds at large in a boundless world!] (172–5)

F.R. Leavis reckoned that Percy Bysshe Shelley had a weak grasp of nature and natural happenings, such as clouds, wind or rain.[44] Leavis objected to Shelley's breathless language, his over–use of words such as *radiant, faint, sweet* and *winged*. The same criticism can be levelled at Friedrich Hölderlin, who also over–uses terms such as *light, beautiful, breeze, heaven,* and *gold.* Throughout Hölderlin's poetry a cool wind blows, a wind from Greece, while a furious West wind blows throughout Shelley's verse, a wind from ancient Rome. In Hölderlin's poesie we are

---

44 F. R. Leavis: *Revaluation: Tradition and Development in English Poetry,* Chatto & Windus 1949, and in M. H. Abrams, 1975

always made aware of heaven, a radiant heaven, not the Catholic place where St Peter waits at them Pearly Gates, but a heaven of the gods, an Olympia. By the time of Rainer Maria Rilke, this over-arching celestial realm had darkened, and had become a night sky full of stars, as found in the *Duino Elegies*.

At times, Friedrich Hölderlin's poesie shines with the light of the Orient, as does the work of Arthur Rimbaud, who often looked towards the East in his poems (specially in *A Season in Hell*). Greece, as Hölderlin knew, stands at the gateway to India and the East, and Hölderlin's heavenly skies are symbols of an otherness that is Oriental. In 'Der Archipelagus' ('The Archipelago'), Hölderlin conjures up an exotic landscape which blooms under the light of Asia: this incredible poem begs to be read aloud:

> And the heavenly, too, the powers up above us, the silent,
> Who from afar bring the cloudless day, delicious sleep and forebodings
> Down to the heads of sentient mortals, bestowing
> Gifts in their fullness and might, they too, your playmates as ever,
> Dwell with you as before, and often in evening's glimmer
> When from Asia's mountains the holy moonlight comes drifting
> In and the stars commingle and meet in your billows,
> With a heavenly brightness you shine, and just as they circle
> So do your waters turn, and the theme of your brothers, their night song
> Vibrant up there, re-echoes lovingly here in your bosom.
> When the all-transfiguring, then, she, the child of the Orient,
> Miracle-worker, the sun of our day-time, is present,
> All that's alive in a golden dream recommences,
> Golden dream the poetic one grants us anew every morning,
> Then to you, the sorrowing god, she will send a still gladder
> enchantment,
> And her own beneficent light is not equal in beauty
> To the token of love, the wreath, which even now and as ever
> Mindful of you, she winds round your locks that are greying.
> Does not Aether enfold you, too, and your heralds, the clouds, do
> They not return to you with his gift, the divine, with the rays that
> Come from above? And then you scatter them over the country
> So that drunken with thunderstorms woods on the sweltering coastline
> Heave and roar as you do, and soon like a boy playing truant,
> Hearing his father call out, with his thousand sources meander

Hurries back from his wanderings and from his lowlands Kayster
Cheering rushes towards you, and even the first-born, that old one
Who too long lay hidden, your Nile, the imperious, majestic,
Haughtily striding down from the distant peaks, as though armed with
Clanging weapons, victorious arrives, and longs to enfold you.

Yet you think yourself lonely; at night in the silence the rock hears
Your repeated lament, and often, winged in their anger,
Up to heaven away from mortals your waves will escape you.
For no longer they live beside you, these noble beloved ones
Who revered you, who once with beautiful temples and cities
Wreathed your shores; and always they seek it and miss it,
Always, as heroes need garlands, the hallowed elements likewise
Need the hearts of us men to feel and to mirror their glory. (215)

Friedrich Hölderlin is a 'poet's poet', in the sense that he creates 'pure poetry', poetry which does not require footnotes or explications, poetry which comes from individual feeling and thought, poetry which, though it is a product of its time and fashion, as all art is, strikes out of its own, carving its own niche in the cultural fabric of the West, poetry which builds on pure lyricism, poetry which, despite his later madness, remains passionate and authentic, imbued with the authenticity of the artist creating at the height of his/ her powers.

But he was humble in discussing his own work. In the preface to *Friedensfeier*, Friedrich Hölderlin writes:

> All I ask is that the reader be kindly disposed towards these pages. In that case he will certainly not find them incomprehensible, far less objectionable. But if, nonetheless, some should think such a language too conventional, I must confess to them: I cannot help it. On a fine day – they should consider – almost every mode of song makes itself heard; and Nature, whence it originates, also receives it again.[45]

With its marvellously direct lines, such as the opening of 'Der Ister' ('The Ister'): 'Now come, fire!' (493), Friedrich Hölderlin's poetry comes from a realm of metaphysical and mythological splendour, and goes towards that cultural space of splendour with

---

45 F. Hölderlin, quoted in Michael Hamburger, *Reason*, 30.

more assurance than the work of most poets.

Friedrich Hölderlin, like Johann Wolfgang von Goethe or John Keats, is not afraid to make massive statements, for when he is heated up in his shamanic fire, as with Arthur Rimbaud or Dante Alighieri, Hölderlin goes straight for the mark, and usually reaches it. As in 'The Poet's Courage', one of his finest short pieces:

Sind denn dir nicht verwandt alle Lebendigen?
    Nährt zum Dienste denn nicht selber die Parze dich?
        Drum! so wandle nur wehrlos
            Fort durch's Leben und sorge nicht!

Was geschiehet, es sei alles geseegnet dir,
    Sei zur Freude gewandt! oder was könnte denn
        Dich belaidigen, Herz! was
            Da begegnen, wohin du sollst?

Denn, wie still am Gestad, oder in silberner
    Fernhintönender Fluth, oder auf schweigenden
        Wassertiefen der leichte
            Schwimmer wandelt, so sind auch wir,

Wir, die Dichter des Volks, gerne, wo Lebendes
    Um uns athmet und wallt, freudig, und jedem hold,
        Jedem trauend; wie sängen
            Sonst wir jedem den eignen Gott?

Wenn die Wooge denn auch einen der Muthigen,
    Wo er treulich getraut, schmeichlend hinunterzieht,
        Und die Stimme des Sängers
            Nun in blauender Halle schweigt;

Freudig starb er und noch klagen die Einsamen,
    Seine Haine, den Fall ihres Geliebtesten;
        Öfters tönet der Jungfrau
            Vom Gezweige sein freundlich Lied.

Wenn des Abends vorbei Einer der Unsern kömmt,
    Wo der Bruder ihm sank, denket er manches wohl
        An der warnenden Stelle,
            Schweigt und gehet gerüsteter.

[Is not all that's alive close and akin to you,
  Does the Fate not herself keep you to serve her ends?
    Well, then, travel defenceless
      On through life, and fear nothing there!

All that happens there be welcome, be blessed to you,
  Be an adept in joy, or is there anything
    That could harm you there, heart, that
      Could offend you, where you must go?

For, as quiet near shores, or in the silvery
  Flood resounding afar, or over silent deep
    Water travels the flimsy
      Swimmer, likewise we love to be

Where around us there breathe, teem those alive, our kind,
  We, their poets; and glad, friendly to every man,
    Trusting all. And how else for
      Each of them could we sing his god?

Though the wave will at times, flattering, drag below
  One such brave man where, true, trusting he makes his way,
    And the voice of that singer
      Now falls mute as the hall turns blue;

Glad he died there, and still lonely his groves lament
  Him whom most they had loved, lost, though with joy he
                                                    drowned;
    Often a virgin will hear his
      Kindly song in the distant boughs.

When at nightfall a man like him, of our kind, comes
  Past the place where he sank, many a thought he'll give
    To the site and the warning,
      Then in silence, more armed, walk on.] (204-7)

4

HEINE

Our lyrical poetry is a product of spiritualism, although its material is sensualistic, the longing of the isolated mind to be merged with the world of phenomena, to mingle with nature. As sensualism triumphs, lyrical poetry must end, for there arises a longing for the spiritual: sentimentality, which grows ever thinner and fainter, nihilistic mawkishness, a hollow fog of verbiage, a halfway house between has-been and will-be, tendentious poetry.

Heinrich Heine, epitaph[46]

Heinrich Heine wrote all manner of poems, from topical and political pieces to meditations of Hebraic culture and Christianity. He created all manner of texts and books, from studies of the Romantic era to lyrical poems.[47] He was one of the late Romantics, and wrote critically and ironically of his Romantic forebears in *Der romantische Schule*.[48] This reading of Heine's work will concentrate

---

46 H. Heine, quoted in Michael Hamburger: *Reason and Energy*, 161
47 See Jeffrey L. Samons: *Heinrich Heine: A Modern Biography*, Princeton University Press, 1979, and his *Heinrich Heine: The Elusive Poet*, Yale University Press, New Haven 1969; S.S. Pawer, 1961; Barker Fairley: *Heinrich Heine: An Interpretation*, Clarendon Press 1963; A.I. Sandor: *The Exile of Gods*, Mouton, The Hague, 1967
48 H. Heine: *Der romantische Schule*, Sämtlichte Werke, vol.3, ed. Klaus Briegleb, Hanser, Munich 1971

on his lyrical poetry, in particular his love poetry.[49] Love is a central experience in Romanticism, as I have maintained in this book. Friedrich Schlegel, of whom Heine was very critical, wrote that love 'is an intimation of the higher, the infinite, a hieroglyph of the one eternal love, of the sacred, life–abundance of creative nature'.[50] There is not space to discuss his satirical work, his political writings,[51] his relation with British culture,[52] his relation to Jewish culture,[53] and the elements of philosophy and mythology in his poetry.[54]

Christian Johann Heinrich Heine was born in Düsseldorf on December 13, 1797 and died in Paris on February 17, 1856. Some of Heine's best-known works were *Briefe aus Berlin, Almansor, William Ratcliff, Lyrisches Intermezzo, Reisebilder, The North Sea, Book of Songs, Der Salon, Shakespeares Mädchen und Frauen, New Poems, Atta Troll: Ein Sommernachtstraum, Der Doktor Faust,* and *Lutezia.* Heine's *Leider* were set to music by, among others, Robert Schumann, Franz Schubert, Felix Mendelssohn, Johannes Brahms, Richard Strauss, Peter Tchaikovsky, and Richard Wagner.

Like Francesco Petrarch and William Shakespeare, Heinrich Heine was a very self–conscious poet, conscious of the function and poetics of poetry, and its reception by an audience. He was aware of his audience, and cultivated a relationship with his audience, as his Prefaces show, and as comments such as this from the Postscript to *Romancero*: 'An author winds up by getting used to his public as if it were a rational being.'[55]

Heinrich Heine's work displays many ambiguities; there is an ambivalence at the heart of his poetry, as he simultaneously explores and sends up poetic methods and ideas. He is a poet who

49 See S.S. Pawer, 1960
50 Friedrich Schlegel, II, 334
51 See William Ross: *Heinrich Heine: Two Studies of His Thought and Feeling,* Clarendon Press 1956; Nigel Reeves: *Heinrich Heine: Poetry and Politics,* Oxford University Press, 1974
52 See S.S. Pawer, 1986
53 See S.S. Pawer, 1983; Israel Tabak: *Judaic Lore in Heine,* John Hopkins Press, Baltimore, 1948
54 See Robert C. Holub: *Heinrich Heine's Reception of German Grecophilia,* Heidelberg 1981
55 H. Heine: *Complete Poems,* 696

shifts his goals continually, who does not remain fixed in one poetic stance. His early poetry, like that of so many young poets, is full of fervour, emotion and idealism. It is mainly love poetry, this early work, as with Dante Alighieri or William Shakespeare.

Heinrich Heine sings breathlessly of love, of love won and lost, of love, above all, *desired*, so that desire itself is really Heine's subject. Heine is in love with love, not really with the beloved. Love poetry becomes for him, as for Francesco Petrarch and the Italian *stilnovisti,* an elegant mirror that reflects back, as in the myth of Narcissus, his own desire. Poetry is a narcissistic mirror, in which the poet sees his love reflected. His love obscures the beloved woman; she is a springboard, merely, for his artistic excesses. 'To the lover she is the ultimate reality', writes Novalis in his philosophical fragments.[56] We see this so clearly in Dante Alighieri's *Vita Nuova*, where Beatrice Portinari is simply a pretext for poetry, or with Francesco Petrarch and his Laura de Noyes. In Petrarch's *Rime Sparse*, the true 'subject' of the poetry is not Laura but Petrarch himself, the creation of a poem, endlessly polished, honed, shaped, sculpted, cultivated, refined. The troubadour Giraut de Borneil spoke of polishing one's songs (*cansos*) so they would shine, reflecting back his love.

Heinrich Heine's poetry is fiercely heterosexual, as is Francesco Petrarch's or Thomas Hardy's or Edmund Spenser's (Bill Shakespeare, John Donne and Percy Shelley, though, consciously explored the boundaries of gender). Heine loves women, like Robert Graves or Bernard de Ventadour. 'A woman's body is a song', he wrote in 'The Song of Songs',

God writes it with His Word
In nature's grandest album when
His spirit once was stirred. (743)

Heinrich Heine's early poetry, in the *Book of Songs*, is a mass of seething, youthful, inspired emotions, where the feminine is deeply desired – the erotic as well as spiritual feminine, the

---

56 Novalis: *Pollen and Fragments,* 60

woman who is both spirit (there many fairies and apparitions in Heine, as in John Keats's poetry), and erotic and sensual:

In sweetest dream, in silent night,
She came to me with magic's might,
With magic might, my love–in–bloom,
She came to me, to my own room. (14)

This is from 'Dream Pictures', in *Youthful Sorrows*. The age old scenario of a young man erotically conjuring up visions of female sprites at night occurs throughout Heinrich Heine's early poetry. His mythology of love poetry is archetypal Western erotic art, where the woman, as in the poetry of Maurice Scève and Torquato Tasso, is the Jungian *anima* or feminine soul–image, dressed in white ('the maid was white', Heine writes, 12). The archetypal three colours of poetry occur here, the colours of alchemy and magic: black, white and red. Black is the night, the poet's unconscious, 'Mother Night', the all–encompassing world–space or World–Soul out of which the female spirit comes, dressed in white, her face radiant, her eyes shining, her very illumination pierces the poet, and, out of this combination of black and white comes red, the red of blood throbbing and pulsing in sexual arousal ('My blood is wild', Heine writes, 130), the red of passion ('In burning words my passing lows', 15), heat, burning fever and religious intoxication. These three colours, and variations of them, occur throughout love poetry (in Beatrice's red dress in Dante Alighieri's dream in the *Vita Nuova*, for instance, in the colour of countless blushing cheeks in the works of the troubadours, *Minnesängers*, minstrels and *stilnovisti*).

She, the beloved, the desired woman, the Goddess, is a spectre, a phantom, a ghost, a demon. The poet does not realize he has wished her up, like a magician. Magic flows throughout Heinrich Heine's early verse, as it does in William Shakespeare (*A Midsummer Night's Dream* and *Love's Labour's Lost*, for instance). Magic is that stuff that enables the spirit–woman to appear, that allows the poet to speak of such things, that encourages the shamanic night journeys of the dreaming artist/ autist. Dreaming is central to Heine's poetry:

> When I lie on my pallet,
> Embraced by night, I trace
> Hovering there before me
> An image of sweet grace. (96)

Heinrich Heine, like so many poets before and after him, acknowledged the notion of the poet as shaman, the poet as wish-fulfilling magician. Indeed, Heine identified with Merlin the magician, as William Shakespeare's Prospero did (with more than a hint of John Dee thrown in, in Prospero's case). In the Postscript to *Romancero*, when he was bed-ridden – he called the bed his 'mattress-grave' – Heine identified with Merlin being emprisoned late in his life:

> My body has shrivelled so much that almost nothing is left but the voice, and my bed reminds me of the tolling grave of the magician Merlin, which lies in the forest of Brozeliand in Brittany, under tall oaks whose tops shoot up to heaven like green flames. Ah, I envy you, dear colleague Merlin, these trees and the fresh breezes blowing through them, for there is not a single green leaf rustling here in my mattress-grave in Paris. (693)

Merlin the magician was, legend has it, imprisoned by the enchantress Nimue. Merlin was a slave, ultimately, of the feminine power and mysteries, as was Prospero, who got all his magical powers from the Witch Sycorax. Prospero lived in the domain of the Eternal Feminine, as did Faust and Merlin. They drew on the Goddess for their powers. Heinrich Heine, too, can be seen as a Goddess-orientated poet, a 'Muse-poet', to use Robert Graves' terminology, a poet who lived in the thrall of his Muse, a woman both real and spiritual, both erotic and æthereal. In 'Katharina', Heine wrote:

> Like sage Merlin, I am bound
> By the magic spell I wrought;

In the end I'm snared and caught
On my own enchanted ground. (358)

Maurice Scève was enslaved by Délie, or Sir Philip Sidney's Astrophel with Stella, or William Shakespeare with the fair youth, or Edmund Spenser with Gloriana, and so on.

Heinrich Heine's early poetry, especially in his *Book of Songs*, can be seen as Goddess poetry. In the Preface to the second edition, Heine wrote:

> …first of all come songs which were written in those earlier years when the first kisses of the German muse were burning in my soul. Ah, the kisses of that excellent wench have since lost much of their ardor and freshness! Under such long–standing conditions the fervency of the honeymoon is bound to cool down gradually, but tenderness often becomes so much the more deeply felt, especially on bad days, and thus it was the German muse showed me all of her love and fidelity! (4–5)

You can find the Muse or the Goddess in most places in Heinrich Heine's poetry, not just in the *Book of Songs*. There are many poems to particular women, for instance: Seraphine, Psyche, The Unknown She, Katharina, Friedrike, Emma, Clarisse, Hortense, Diana, Angelique, real and mythical women, written in the middle period.

In the *Lyrical Intermezzo*, Heinrich Heine wrote of the archetypal dream–woman:

> Then in glides his loved one, in shimmering clothes
> Of sea foam mantling her graces;
> She flows and glows like a blossoming rose,
> Her veil is of jewelled laces.
> Her golden hair flutters around her pale form,
> Her sweet eyes invite him, passionate, warm –
> They fall in each other's embraces. (51)

The dream–woman here is an archetypal erotic object, at once sensual and spiritual, anchored by allusions to roses, one of *the* symbols prime of the Eternal Feminine, a symbol which combines love and death in multi–faceted ways. Other usual trappings of spiritual–women are here: the images of light (golden hair, shimmering clothes), the seductive eyes, images of heat (the warm embrace), the flowing, sensuous movements, the allusions to the appearance of Venus rising from the sea (sea foam), and the veil. Veils have to be pierced or drawn aside by the errant knight, who is the questing phallic male; he has to move beyond each layer to get to the heart of the woman, her spiritual and sexual centre, which is her vulva (symbolized in so many poets by the rose).

Like much Romantic poetry, Heinrich Heine's is very erotic – not simply sensual, but deeply erotic. As when he writes of the beloved's mouth:

> Her red mouth, rich and velvety
> Gave me a kiss that set my lips aglow (49)

Thomas Hardy wrote similarly erotically of Tess's mouth in *Tess of the d'Urbervilles*. Or when Heine links love and pain in the kiss of a lover (recalling the *mors osculis*, kiss of death of occultism):

> You hurt my lips with kisses, so
> Now kiss the pain away (174)

For Heinrich Heine, lying in the embrace of a lover's arms is the way to heaven, as with the troubadours and *Minnesängers* (an early poem in *Book of Songs* was entitled 'The Minnesingers'). The troubadours might prefer to say 'lying between a woman's legs' rather than, in the Romantic, more fastidious fashion, 'in a lover's embrace'. For Heine, spiritual and sexual ecstasy fuse, and the lover's embrace enables religious rapture:

> When she embraced me, tenderly clinging,
> My soul flew heavenward, flew straight up! (174)

Or again, lyrics from *Lyrical Intermezzo*:

Beloved woman, embrace me
With love encompassing;
Let your arms and legs enlace me,
Your supple body cling. (171)

It's all there in Heinrich Heine's poetry, the merging of the
sensual and the spiritual, where the flesh–and–blood beloved
merges into various incarnations of the spiritual or fairy woman.
In the art of Dante Alighieri and Francesco Petrarch, Beatrice and
Laura merge into the Virgin Mary, as also in John Donne and
Edmund Spenser. In Heine's poetry, the beloved is compared to
an angel, a fairy, a spirit, and so on. In *Lyrical Intermezzo*, she is
compared to that holy of holies in Arthurian romance, the Holy
Grail (53), which as Jungians remind us, is a fount or cauldron of
feminine mysteries, a world–womb out of which flows life itself.

And so Heinrich Heine goes on to draw together heaps of
mediæval imagery, floral symbolism (eyes like violets), Christian
mysticism (embodied by cathedrals, the Virgin Mary), Classical
mythology ('foam born child of ocean', 57), and *stilnovisti* conceits
(sweet eyes, sweet lips, sweet cheeks, eyes like flowers, cheeks of
red roses, hands like white lilies, 61).

Heinrich Heine's *Book of Songs* is essentially a story of desire,
desire felt and thwarted, as in Johann Wolfgang von Goethe's
Faust or *Young Werther,* or Novalis' *Hymns To the Night*. Desire
suffuses most of Heine's poetry, as it does with William
Shakespeare's plays or D.H. Lawrence's novels. The *Book of Songs*
depicts many scenes of weeping, pathetic tears and claspings,
partings, or sitting alone on the beach, at sunset ('We sat in the
lonely fisher's shack,/ We sat there silent, alone', he writes in *The
Homecoming*, 82). A recurring theme in Heine's output is the
vision of female visitors to the dreaming man by night, the sprites
who appear in erotic embraces with the sleeping knight, as in
'Dream and Life' from *Youthful Sorrows*, where fairies dance
around him (169).

The North Sea cycle of poems (inspired by Heinrich Heine's
visits to Norderney, an East Frisian Island, in 1825–27), presents

the archetypal Romantic situation, depicted in a number of different ways but all basically revolving around Romantic subjectivity. Heine creates the typical Poet Alone scenario: the poet at night on a windswept beach. The image has all the ingredients of Romanticism: the sense of the infinite in the spaces of sea; light and dark (stars shining amidst black night); feminine mysteries (night itself, the fecund ocean, etc); solitude and subjectivity; the aristocratic ego against the world; desire, which comes from the space around the poet, the distance between him and what he desires, the vast space indicating his separateness from other people, in particular the beloved woman; nature – lots of nature in that sea and sky's motion – the sea *never* stops moving; ecstasy – the poet feeling ecstatic being alone beside the ocean; mysticism – being alone amidst nature allows the poet to muse upon pantheism and the One and All; religious unity – the poet sees the Oversoul or World–Soul in all things, sees all things as one, and himself at the centre of everything. All these things are expressed in Heine's poet alone on the beach beside the North Sea: this is all of the poem 'Declaration':

> All dusked in shadow came the evening,
> Wilder tumbled the waves,
> And I sat on the shores and gazed at
> The white dance of the billows,
> And my heart swelled up like the sea,
> And a longing seized me, deep homesickness
> For you, the lovely image
> That everywhere haunts me
> And everywhere calls to me,
> Everywhere, everywhere,
> In the howl of the wind, in the growl of the sea,
> And in the sighing of my own breast.
> With slender reed I wrote on the sand,
> "Agnes, I love you!"
> But cruel waves washed in
> Over the sweet confession
> And blotted it out.
>
> You fragile reed, you crumbling sand,

You fugitive waves, I trust you no more!
The heavens grow darker, my heart grows wilder,
And with mighty hand, from Norway's forests
I wrench the tallest fir tree
And dip it deep
Into Etna's burning maw, and with this
Fiery-tipped pen of giants
I write on the darkling dome of heaven,
"Agnes, I love you!"

Every night since then they burn
Up there, the eternal words of flame,
And all the children of men to come
Will joy to read the heavenly words:
"Agnes, I love you!" (137)

The poet alone on the windy strand feels ecstasy but still feels a
lack, and a desire. There is still the beloved woman, in his past
and perhaps in his future, which he has not conquered. We see
Heinrich Heine's poet here making a massive gesture, painting
his love in fire on the heavens, verily an act of Promethean-like
proportions. It is an out-size performance, bigger than art, a
mythic act.

No, the poet, no matter how self-contained he may be in his
subjectivity, still yearns for the beloved woman. So, when he
looks at the stars, he sees her eyes, he gasps:

They're her eyes, the stars up yonder,
My love's eyes
(in 'A Night in the Cabin', 138)

Heinrich Heine simultaneously mocks this yearning Romantic
tradition even as he exalts it. Restlessness is his hallmark as a
poet, in one sense, as it is of Percy Shelley. More interesting is
when Heine moves off the subject of love, and thrills to the
splendours of nature. He can be an extraordinary nature poet, as
mystical and powerful as the best of them (William Wordsworth,
Johann Wolfgang von Goethe, Emily Dickinson). In 'Ship-
wrecked' Heine conjures up the notion of a 'black sun' (central to

D.H. Lawrence's mythopœia):

O my jet–black sun how often –
How thrilling–often I drank from you
Wild flames of inspiration,
And stood and reeled, as if drunk with fire,
And then a dove–mild smile came hovering
About your proud full–curving lips
And your proud full–curving lips
Breathed out words as sweet as moonlight
And tender as roses' fragrance –
And my soul was lifted up
And soared like an eagle up to the heavens! (148)

Heinrich Heine is well aware of the pitfalls of being so rapturous in poetry, and much of his rapture is in fact irony. For Karl Kraus, Heine's poetry was imitation, a synthetic Romanticism.[57] The problem is the distinctions between irony and straight–faced poetry are not always made clear, and an ambivalence abounds in his work. His attitudes to women, for instance, are fraught with loathing as well as love. In Heine's poetry, as in the art of Goethe, Novalis, Hölderlin, Drayton, de Musset and any male poet you care to mention, there is an ambiguous attitude towards women and things 'feminine'. Fear and desire are the twin poles of Heine's work, as of so many poets' work. So that, finally, fear and desire express themselves in an ironic mode, which knows full well how art digs its own grave. Or as Heine puts it in a short lyric:

Day and night I've poetized,
Yet gained nothing that I prized;
Though my harmony's unsurpassed,
This has got me nowhere fast. (277)

Francesco Petrarch and William Shakespeare too knew well how the very act of writing complicates and adds to the problem it is trying to grapple with. Thus, writing about love is therapy on one

---

57 Karl Kraus: *Mein Gutachten*, in *Literature and Lüge*, Munich 1962, 39–41

level. It deals with feelings of loss and yearning. On another level, though, writing of love simply exaggerates the fact that one is *not in love*, or with the beloved right at that moment. For, if one were in love (or lying beside the beloved), one would not be writing about love. Henri Matisse spoke of painting in the same way: 'I too have said one wouldn't paint if one were happy. I'm in agreement with Picasso on that one. We have to live over a volcano.'[58] If one was really happy, one would not write poetry. Art, it seems, comes out of dissatisfaction, an ontological restlessness. We see this so clearly in the Romantics, in Percy Bysshe Shelley or Heinrich Heine, John Keats or Friedrich Schlegel. J. P. Stern writes:

> If there is one theme which German poets of the last three centuries have made peculiarly and poignantly their own, it is their concern with the world as a place of insecurity and impermanence, a provisional state...[59]

Heinrich Heine thrives on restlessness, on argument, on Hegelian dialectical discourse. For instance, he writes in the *Romancero* Postscript: 'Yes, I have returned to God, like the prodigal son, after a long time of tending swine with the Hegelians.' (695)

It is not simply a question of a dualism of ethics where spirituality is on one side and sensuality on the other, for, as Michael Hamburger notes, '"sensualism" too was a religion' (*Reason*, 149). Heinrich Heine's cult of sensuality contains contradictions, not least with Judæo–Christianity, which constituted the 'religion of pain' as Heine termed it. Like Oswald Spengler in *The Decline of the West*, Heine regarded the Christian era as a disease, a falling away, a decay of world culture after the ecstasy and refinement of ancient Greece. Or as he put it in *Memoirs of Herr von Schnabelewopski*: 'Our age – and it begins at the Cross of Christ – will be regarded as a great period of human illness.'[60]

58 H. Matisse, quoted in Pierre Schneider: Matisse, Rizzoli, New York 1984, 734
59 J. Stern: *The Heart of Europe: Essays on Literature and Ideology*, Blackwell 1992, 307
60 H. Heine: *Works*, 1, 545

Heinrich Heine seems to be accurate here, but this was by no means Heine's fixed view. His views often changed. Sensuality, in Heine's view, becomes a part of a pantheistic Christianity, if it is not already too contradictory to put pantheism and Christianity together. Indeed, William Wordsworth and the English Romantics readily fused Christianity and pantheism, speaking on the one hand of the Christian Father–God, and on the other hand of the 'One and All', the 'world–soul' or Oversoul that pervades everything, that is and is not the Judæo–Christian God. Heine wrote:

> Sounds and words, colours and shapes, sensuous phenomena of every kind are only symbols of an idea, symbols that arise in the artist's mind when it is moved by the holy World Spirit; his works of art are only symbols by which he communicates his own ideas to other minds.[61]

One can take all of Heinrich Heine's poetry as parody and irony, but then, not many writers create hundreds of pages of mockery without also having something of the attitude of the 'erotic irony' that Thomas Mann spoke about, where the mocker actually loves what is being mocked (otherwise, what would be the point? Why waste so much time writing so much poetry if one hates everything about one's subject?). In Heine's love poetry, despite the parodies and imitations, there is an undercurrent of desire that seems to be authentic. A yearning that parody cannot erase. There is, under the sarcasm and bile, gentle thoughts at times, an idealism in Heine's poetry, even a utopianism, which surfaces from time to time, as in this famous extract from his *History*:

> Happier and more beautiful generations, conceived in rarely chosen embraces, who grow up in a religion of joy, will smile sorrowfully at their poor ancestors, who gloomily abstained from all the pleasures of this fair earth, and, by deadening their warm and colourful senses, were reduced almost to chilly spectres. Yes, I saw it with certainty, our descendants will be happier and more beautiful than we. For I believe in progress, I believe that mankind is destined to be happy, and thus I

---

61 Quoted in M. Hamburger: *Reason*, 156

think more highly of divinity than those pious people who think mankind was created only to suffer. Here on earth, by the blessings of free political and industrial institutions, I should like to establish that bliss which, in the opinion of the pious, will come only in heaven, on the day of judgment.[62]

---

62 H. Heine: *Works*, 3, 518–9

4

NOVALIS

Poetry is what is truly and absolutely real, this is the kernel of my philosophy. The more poetic, the more true.

Novalis[63]

Novalis is the most mystical of the German Romantic poets. He is at once the most typical and the most unusual of the German Romantic poets – indeed, of all Romantic poets.[64] He is supremely idealistic, far more so than Johann Wolfgang von Goethe or Heinrich Heine. He died young, which makes him, like Percy Bysshe Shelley and John Keats, something of a hero (or martyr). He did not write as much as Shelley, but his work, like that of Keats or Arthur Rimbaud, promised much. For Michael Hamburger, Novalis' work is almost totally idealistic:

> Novalis's philosophy, then, is not mystical, but utopian. That is why his imaginative works are almost wholly lacking in conflict. They are a perpetual idyll.[65]

63 Novalis: *Works* (Minor), III, 11
64 See Richard Faber, 1970; Heinz Ritter: "Die geistlichen Lieder des Novalis. Ihre Datierung und Entstehung", *Jahrbuch der deutschen Schiller-Gesellschaft*, IV, 1960, 308–42; Friedrich Hiebel: *Novalis*, Francke, Bern 1972; Curt Grutzmacher, 1964; Géza von Molnár, 1970; John Neubauer, 1972; Bruce Haywood, 1959.
65 M. Hamburger: *Reason and Energy*, 97

It's true, Novalis' work is supremely idealistic, and utopian. But it is also mystical, because it points towards the invisible, unseen, unknown, and aims to reach that ecstatic realm. He wrote:

> The sense of poetry has much in common with that for mysticism. It is the sense of the peculiar, personal, unknown, mysterious, for what is to be *revealed*, the necessary-accidental. It represents the unrepresentable. It sees the invisible, feels the unfeelable, etc... The sense for poetry has a close relationship with the sense for augury and the religious sense, with the sense for prophecy in general.[66]

Novalis was born Georg Philipp Friedrich von Hardenberg on May 2, 1772 in Oberwiederstedt. He studied law between 1790 and 1794 at Jena, Wittenberg and Leipzig. There he met many of the leading literary lights, such as Johann Wolfgang von Goethe, Johann Gottfried Herder, Jean Paul (Johann Paul Friedrich Richter), the Schlegels, Ludwig von Tieck and Friedrich Wilhelm Joseph Schelling. Later, in 1797, Novalis studied at the Mining Academy in Freiburg. He began publishing in 1798. His chief works include: *Faith and Love or the King and the Queen, Pollen, The Novices at Sais, Heinrich von Ofterdingen, Christendom or Europa* and *Hymns To the Night*. He was engaged to Sophie von Kühn from 1794-97, and to Julie von Charpentier from 1798 to his death in 1801. He died on March 25, 1801 in Weißenfels, from tuberculosis.

Novalis was passionately in love with his beloved, Sophie, whom he had met in October, 1794, when she was twelve. They were engaged in March, 1795 (Sophie was 13; Novalis was 22). Novalis was devastated when she died on March 19, 1797, two days after her fifteenth birthday. 'My main task should be', he wrote, 'to bring everything into a relationship to [Sophia's] idea.'[67] After the death of Sophie von Kühn, Novalis wrote from Tennstedt, near Grüningen, where she was buried:

> You can imagine [he wrote to Friedrich Schlegel] how I feel in this

66 Novalis: *Novalis Schriften*, 3, 686
67 Novalis: ib, 4, 37

neighbourhood, the old witness of my and her glory. I still feel a secret enjoyment to be so close to her grave. It attracts me ever more closely, and this now occasionally constitutes my indescribable happiness. My autumn has come, and I feel so free, usually so vigorous – something can come of me after all. This much I solemnly assure you as become absolutely clear to me what a heavenly accident her death has been – the key to everything – a marvellously appropriate event. Only through it could various things be absolutely resolved and much immaturity overcome. A simple mighty force has come to reflection within me. My love has become a flame gradually consuming everything earthly.[68]

Sophie von Kühn he was for Novalis something like Dante Alighieri's Beatrice or Francesco Petrarch's Laura, or Maurice Scève's Délie; that is, a soul–image or *anima* figure, someone pure and holy. Further, Sophie the person fused for Novalis with 'Sophia' of Gnostic philosophy, the Goddess about whom C.G. Jung has written so eloquently.

> My favourite study [wrote Novalis in 1796] has the same name as my fiancée. Sophie is her name – philosophy is the soul of my life and the key to my innermost self. Since that acquaintance, I also have become completely amalgamated with that study.[69]

Sophia is the Goddess of Wisdom; she is an incarnation for poets and mystics of the Black Goddess, a deity who presides over the unknown, the dark things, occultism and witchcraft. Novalis was very interested in the occult, in magic and hermeticism, in Neoplatonism, alchemy, theosophy, the *Qabbalah*, and other belief systems. Novalis was fascinated by the 'invisible' realm, the things that are unseen but he knows are there, which is the realm of occultism. As he writes: 'We are bound nearer to the unseen than to the visible.'[70]

Apart from his small collection of lyrics, and his *Hymnen an die Nacht*, one of Novalis' major works was his (unfinished) *Blütenstaub* (*Pollen*) and *Glauben und Liebe* (*Faith and Love*), collections of philosophical fragments. These together form an

---

68 Novalis, in, 4, 220
69 Novalis, letter to Friedrich Schlegel, July 8, 1796, in *Novalis Schriften*, op.cit., 4, 188
70 Novalis: *Pollen and Fragments*, 125

æsthetics of religion, and a mysticism of poetry.

Novalis, like the other (German) Romantics, believed in the magical/ religious unity of the world. For him, all things were united, in one way or another. Novalis was one of the first artists to bring together many seemingly diverse practices and philosophies. Leonardo da Vinci had drawn together botany, biology, anatomy, natural science, engineering, mathematics and other strands of thought in his Renaissance art, and Novalis did the same. The metaphysical synthesis was called *Totalwissenschaft*, a total knowledge.

Novalis learnt much from Friedrich Schlegel, during his time at Jena, one of the centres of German Romanticism. Schlegel wrote at length of the unifying spirit of art, where poetry and philosophy merge: the aim of Romantic poetry, Schlegel wrote, was not only 'to unite all the separate species of poetry and put poetry in touch with philosophy and rhetoric', but also to

> use poetry and prose, inspiration and criticism, the poetry of art and the poetry of nature; and make poetry lively and sociable, and life and society poetic; poeticize wit and fill and saturate the forms of art with every kind of good, solid matters for instruction, and animate them with the pulsation of humour.[71]

Novalis' philosophy may be called 'transcendent philosophy', as his poetry might be called 'transcendent poetry'. He called it 'magisch', 'Magie', his 'magic idealism'.[72] It is a mixture of poetry and philosophy, a poetry of philosophy and a philosophy of poetry.[73] 'Transcendental poetry is an admixture of poetry and philosophy,'[74] he writes. And again: 'Poetry is the champion of philosophy... Philosophy is the theory of poetry.' (ib., 56) Poetry

---

71 F. Schlegel, 1958, 182
72 Novalis: *Works* (Minor), Paris, 1837, III
73 See Manfred Frank: "Die Philosophie des sogenannten "magischen Idealismus"", *Euph*, LXIII, 1969, 88–116; Karl Heinz Volkmann–Schluck: "Novalis' magischer Idealismus", *Die deutsche Romantik*, ed. Hans Steffen, 1967, 45–53; Theodor Haering, 1954; G. Hughes, 66; Manfred Dick: *Die Entwicklung des Gedankens der Poesie in den Fragmenten des Novalis*, Bouvier, Bonn, 1967, 223–77; Hugo Kuhn: *Text und Theorie*, Metzler, Stuttgart 1967
74 Novalis: *Pollen and Fragments*, 57

becomes philosophy, and philosophy becomes poetry. Or as he put it: 'Die Welt wird Traum, der Traum wird Welt' ('World becomes dream, dream becomes world'). Friedrich Schlegel wrote in the *Athenaeum* (fragment 451): 'Universality can attain harmony only through the conjunction of poetry and philosophy'.[75]

Kept by Novalis as a collection of fragments, *Pollen* has affinities with the maxims of Friedrich Nietzsche, the thoughts in Blaise Pascal's *Pensées,* with Jacob Boehme's writings and other mystical collections. It is worth quoting from some of these fragments, which show Novalis at his most idealistic and pithy. His statements summarize the (German) Romantic position on poetry, and the basics of all poetics. First of all, he muses on interiority:

> Toward the Interior goes the arcane way. In us, or nowhere, is the Eternal with its worlds, the past and future... The seat of the world is there, where the inner world and the outer world touch... The inner world is almost more mine than the outer. It is so heartfelt, so private – man is given fullness in that life – it is so native.[76]

Here Novalis heads straight for one of the prime realms of mysticism: the inner world, the life of the spirit, the imagination, the soul. His distinction, and then fusion, of inner and outer is the beginnings of modern psychology. It is also one of the key aspects of poetry. For the poet, the inner, psychic or spiritual world is as real and as important, and nourishing, as the outer, public world. The two in fact are part of a continuum, both flowing into each other, like the *yin–yang* dualism of Chinese mysticism. The one informs the other in art. They are not separated, that is the key point. They form a unity. As Novalis wrote in his poem 'Know Yourself' (the title comes from the basic tenet of Greek hermeticism): 'There is only one'.[77]

In magic and hermeticism, the fundamental tenet is 'as above, so below', which, in the modern era, becomes the psychological 'as outside, so inside'. Poets have long known about this

---

75 F. Schlegel, *Lucinde and the Fragments*, 240
76 Novalis: *Pollen and Fragments*, 50-53
77 Novalis: *Pollen and Fragments*, 137

inside-outside pairing. In William Shakespeare's plays, the external setting of a scene – the opening of *Macbeth*, for instance – indicates the characters' inner feelings. Further, in Shakespeare's Elizabethan theatre, there were few props, and little scenery on stage, so the words became full of images, painting pictures in the audience's mind. Hence, in a different way, inner and outer became fused.

For Novalis, rightly, the seat of the soul is precisely that poetic space where 'the inner world and the outer world touch' (150). It was Rainer Maria Rilke who fully developed this inner-outer unity in his lyrics. Rilke is, as we have said, the poet most like Novalis in German poetry. Rilke had his notion of the Angel (in the *Duino Elegies*). The Rilkean Angel is essentially a shaman, and Novalis also speaks at length in his various collections of fragments of the poet as shaman. He does not use the term 'shaman', but his 'sorcerer' or 'genius' or 'prophet' is basically the archaic shaman, the angelic traveller to other worlds, the vatic mouthpiece of his/ her cult, the dancing, drumming, musical figure, like Dionysius or Orpheus, who knows how to fly, who can climb the World Tree, who can penetrate the invisible.[78] Novalis writes:

> The sorcerer is a poet. The prophet is to the sorcerer as the man of taste is to the poet… The genuine poet is all-knowing… (50-1)

As Weston La Barre notes, there is not much difference between the artist, the genius, the criminal, the psychotic and the mad person. Novalis writes:

> Madness and magic have many similarities. A magician is an artist of madnesses. (79)

Similarly, William Shakespeare wrote in *A Midsummer Night's Dream*: 'The lunatic, the lover and the poet,/ Are of imagination all compact.' (V.i.7) In Shakespeare's art, there are deep

---

78 See Mircea Eliade, 1975; *Shamanism*, 1972; Weston La Barre, 1972

connections between lovers, lunatics, poets – and fools. They are all caught up with some kind of 'madness', some kind of 'abnormal', 'extraordinary' subjectivity. Their goals may be different, but they are all connected psychologically. Similarly, for Novalis, as for so many poets, love can be seen as a 'madness', and there is a narrow dividing line between the religious maniac and the fool. There is the 'holy fool' figure in Russian history, the 'trickster god' in ancient mythology, and King Lear's clown, the court jester who is allowed to transgress the boundaries that others are not allowed to cross. St Paul, after all, veered from madness to mysticism, and before his conversion and sainthood was an extremely unlikeable, morally dubious creature.[79]

Novalis as a poet sees the unity of all things, so he writes: 'All barriers are only there for the traversing' (87). This is the Romantic poet talking here: this is a very Romantic notion, it seems, this perception that barriers are there to be transgressed. This is the poet as social rebel speaking, knowing that art must go to extremes. Thus, madness, poetry, idiocy, genius and love form a continuum which is life itself.

In Novalis's *œuvre*, love and mysticism, the secular and the sacred, art and religion, fuse. Thus, in Novalis' 'magic idealism', we hear of the mysticism of love, or the religious nature of art. In this he is no different from other Romantics, such as William Wordsworth or Victor Hugo. For Novalis, life itself is sacred. 'Our whole life is a divine service', he writes (124). In this Novalis is in

---

79 Weston La Barre writes: 'The apostle Paul was a pathetically unprepossessing man, small, bow legged, blind in one eye, and he apparently also suffered from a slight deformity of the trunk. He had a speech defect, was epileptic, and had violently murdered his brother while in an evidently epileptic–equivalent state, and on his own testimony had severe sexual problems (Romans, 7:14). He was unmarried and had nothing sexually to do with women, whom he hated and feared, although he accepted money, food and shelter from them. In personality, Paul was doctrinaire and bigoted... Paul...achieved only a paranoid identification of the divine Hebraic Father with the divinized Hellenistic Son; it is his own pathology projected... Paul was quite familiar with the platonic Noble Lie (*Romans*, 3:7) and boldly proclaimed his own: that the Messiah had succeeded by failing, that he had died and not died, that he was actually God sacrificed to God, and that through faith in this new Mystery all mortals would share his immortal godhead. All these fantasies were thoroughly un–Jewish, indeed preposterous and blasphemous in Judaic terms. They were also preposterous and blasphemous in classic Greek terms.' (*The Ghost Dance*, 603, 607–8)

accord with writers such as D.H. Lawrence, who regarded life itself as holy, or the artist and sculptor Eric Gill, or the cult of the Australian aborigines.

The religion of the aborigines is the 'eternal dreamtime', the mythic, timeless state. For them, life was sacred, and life was sacralized by rituals that include singing. The Australian Bushmen speak of 'singing the world into life'. Rainer Maria Rilke wrote in his *Sonnets For Orpheus*: 'song is existence.' The figure of Orpheus, the mythological poet–as–shaman, features prominently, though he is sometimes hidden, in the works of poets such as Novalis (in his story *Heinrich von Ofterdingen*), Rilke and Arthur Rimbaud. Orpheus' song is his art, and his *raison d'être*. Novalis also wrote of music, and its relation to poetry and religion. The notion of the 'music of the spheres', the celestial harmonies that drive the cosmos, is central to Western religion. For Dante Alighieri, God was at the centre of the concentric circles or wheels of the universe. He was at the heart of the *Rosa Mystica*. For Novalis, the 'One' of Neoplatonism now has many names. In Hinduism it is Brahma; in Taoism it is the Tao; in Zen Buddhism it is Pure Reality; in Tibetan mysticism it is the Clear Light of the Void; and in Islam it is Allah.

Simply being alive, as Mircea Eliade notes, was a sacred act:

In the most archaic phases of culture, *to live as a human being* was in itself *a religious act*, since eating, sexual activity, and labour all had a sacramental value. Experience of the sacred is inherent in man's mode of being in the world.[80]

D.H. Lawrence wrote extensively of 'being alive', about real 'livingness'. In *Etruscan Places* he defined it in a way of which Novalis would surely approve:

To the Etruscan all was alive...They [the Etruscans] felt the symbols and danced the sacred dances. For they were always in touch, physically, with the mysteries.[81]

---

80 Mircea Eliade, 1984, 154
81 D.H. Lawrence: *Mornings in Mexico and Etruscan Places,* Penguin 1960, 147–9

Novalis speaks often of 'mysteries' too. For the occult, hermetic, Neoplatonic, religious artist, there must always be some 'mystery' behind everything. No matter how far you go, there must always be something mysterious behind it. It was true for the participants in the Eleusian Mysteries, and it is the same for Romantic poets. The world is not a machine, nor is it limited. It must be infinite, for, behind everything, there is yet more mystery. There are no limits, yet it is the poet's task to find the limits.

Novalis looked back to early Christianity, to Neoplatonism and to Greek religion. Like most Romantics, Novalis was very nostalgic. But he might have looked back also to many Hindu sects, to Tantric cults, to Sufi mystics and poets, to Australian aborigines, to the shamans of Siberia and North America, to the Chinese Taoists (Chuang-tzu, Lao-tzu), or to the Confucians (Confucius, Mencius), or to the Zen masters (Hui-Neng, Dogen, Jakuin), or to the ancient Greeks of Epicurus, Heraclitus or Empodecles' day.

What is the purpose of Novalis' cult of 'transcendent poetry'? More life, basically. This was Rainer Maria Rilke's great goal, his Holy Grail: life and more life, more and more of life. That is our goal, Rilke claimed. Poetry is a way of enabling us to be more alive, say Novalis and Rilke:

Poetry is the great art of constructing transcendental health… Poetry is generation. All compositions must be living individuals. (*Pollen*, 50)

Rainer Maria Rilke says similar things about poetry. In a letter to his Polish translator, Witold von Hulewicz, of November 13, 1925, Rilke explained his notion of the angel: a being that shows us how to be painfully but blissfully alive, living in the transcendent realm of 'the Open', as Rilke called that special poetic place. We must be

Transformed? Yes, for our task is to stamp this provisional, perishing earth into ourselves so deeply, so painfully and passionately, that its being may rise again, "invisibly", in us.[82]

All you have to do in life is to be. Be what, exactly? Just *be*, says Rainer Maria Rilke: 'all we basically have to do is to *be*, but simply, earnestly, the way the earth simply is', he wrote in *Letters on Cézanne*.[83] To simply *be* is really difficult, as Novalis and Rilke admit. Yet it is the goal. To realize, as the Hindu mystics put it, that Thou Art That (*tat tvam asi*). As Novalis wrote:

> Art of becoming all-powerful. Art of realizing our intentions totally. (118)

Total fulfilment – it's a tall order, perhaps, but only this ontological totality will do for Novalis. He is supremely idealistic while at the same being totally honest, and totally simple, and totally ordinary. He is optimistic, it seems, when he writes:

> All is seed. (73)

Yet he is also being quite realistic, knowing, as an artist does, that *anything* can be used in art. A transcendent, total art can include *everything*. Nothing is exempt from art, not even nothingness itself. Indeed, nothingness is a large element of some art (Samuel Beckett's compressed texts, for instance, or Ad Reinhardt's black-on-black paintings), as it is a key component in Buddhism and Taoism.

Novalis' idealistic philosophy is all-inclusive. 'All is seed', he writes. *All.* Or, again, in a different fashion:

> All must become nourishment. (65)

Or, again, in a different way, he says:

> All can become experiment – all can become an organ. (88)

---

82 R.M. Rilke: *Duino Elegies*, tr. J.B. Leishman & Stephen Spender, Hogarth Press, 1957, 157.
83 R.M. Rilke: *Letters on Cézanne*, ed. Clara Rilke, Cape, 1988.

Meister Eckhart, the mediæval mystic whose mystical philosophy is in tune with Rainer Maria Rilke's and Novalis' philosophies, wrote:

The seed of God is in us... The seed of a pear tree grows into a pear tree, a hazel seed into a hazel tree, a seed of God into God.[84]

Much of alchemy, hermeticism, witchcraft, Qabbalism and Neoplatonism is concerned with healing, nourishment and rebirth. It was one of Novalis' chief concerns. The philosophical fragments state the basic view of nourishment in a variety of ways. The fragments are deeply poetic. Although they are written in prose, they are clearly poetry. One of Novalis' most powerful sentences is:

Everything can become magical work. (73)

This statements is itself magical. For Novalis, art is for the enrichment of life. Whatever art may do, Novalis says, it must enrich us. 'To enliven all is the aim of life', he writes (64).

Love features prominently in Novalis' philosophy of poetry and poetry of philosophy. Love – and sex. For, under Novalis' sophisticated sophisms, there is sex. An eroticism which is that fundamental *jouissance* of the text in Romanticism is found in Novalis's work. For Novalis, love and philosophy are aspects of the same mystery. 'It is with love as with philosophy', he writes (*Pollen*, 57). He evokes the *eroticism* of philosophy, something which Plato may have understood subconsciously, but which Novalis brings into the foreground:

In the essential sense, philosophizing is – a caress – a testimony to the inner love of reflection, the absolute delight of wisdom. (53)

For Novalis, the highest form of love is spiritual, of course. In

---

84 Quoted in James M. Clark & John V. Skinner: *Meister Eckhart*, London 1953, 151.

this he is in harmony with those other great poets of love, such as Dante Alighieri, Francesco Petrarch, Guido Guinicelli, Guido Cavalcanti and Bernard de Ventadour. For the mediæval troubadours and *stilnovisti*, human love was transcended in stature and significance by spiritual love. In personal terms, this meant that the human, flesh–and–blood beloved, Petrarch's Laura, Dante's Beatrice, Novalis' Sophie, was surpassed, spiritually, and even transcended physically in some cases, by the figure of the Virgin Mary. Novalis too, like Dante and Petrarch, raised the Mother of God above his Sophie as a beloved.

> By absolute will power, love can be gradually transmuted into religion.[85]

This is a familiar pose with (usually male) poets, this worldly renunciation in favour of religious love. 'What I feel for Sophie', Novalis wrote, 'is religion, not love' (ib., 295).

Friedrich Nietzsche had a theory that the more tragic tragedy becomes, the more sensual it becomes. In other words, tragedy has a sensual dimension which increases as the sense of tragedy increases. William Shakespeare's tragedies are his most erotic works. Think of the erotic entanglements of love and death in *Macbeth*, or *King Lear*. Novalis too spoke of the erotic quality of intensity and absolutism. Power is an aphrodisiac, it is said: the powerful people are those who can go to extremes. Tragic characters go to extremes – Macbeth, Beatrice, Othello – they push against their ontological boundaries. They practice a kind of absolutism or extremism that seems particularly Romantic. Novalis notes the sensuality of power and extremism in his fragments, as when he claims:

> All absolute sensation is religious. (197)

Tragic power and political power is sexual and seductive, and so is magical power. Novalis writes:

---

85 Novalis, *Works* (Minor) II, 299

Magic is like art – to wilfully use the sensual realm. (119)

Magicians throughout history have been erotic figures: Aleister Crowley, Georg Gurdjieff, Merlin, Paracelsus. The eroticism of magic is obvious: witchcraft, for instance, was and is regarded very much in sexual terms. Witchcraft was a heresy, certainly, that disturbed the Church for religious reasons, but many of the accusations brought against witchcraft were of a sexual nature.

More 'ordinary' – that is, bourgeois, heterosexual, traditional – are the views of Novalis on love such as this:

Every beloved object is the focus of a paradise… One touches heaven, when one touches a human body. (30, 59)

This neatly summarizes the links between love and religion that have been described throughout history, from the Biblical *Song of Songs* onwards. Novalis says that you touch heaven when you touch a body. This is what the troubadours said, that making love was heavenly, that to enter a woman was to enter heaven. William Shakespeare said it, John Donne said it, John Keats said it, and Robert Graves said it in the British poetic tradition; Sappho and C.P. Cavafy said it in the Greek tradition; Ovid, Dante Alighieri and Giuseppe Ungaretti said it in the Italian tradition; Novalis, Joseph Freiherr von Eichendorff, Ludwig von Tieck and Rainer Maria Rilke said it in the German tradition; Alexander Pushkin, Fyodor Tyutchev, Arseny Tarkovsky and Anna Akhmatova in the Russian tradition.

Not all of Novalis' eroticism was cerebral, philosophic and 'idealistic'. He produced obvious eroticism at times, the sensual love of a beloved which centres on the body:

Wonderful powers of the bodily appearance – the beautiful lineaments – the form – the voice – the complexion – the musculature and elasticity – the eyes, the senses of touch, of feeling – the outer nature – the angles – the closed–off spaces – the darkness – the veil. Through the selection of clothing the body becomes yet more mystical. (116)

In Novalis' *Hymns To the Night*, the night itself is a vast, erotic, maternal, deep, dazzling space, the place of Henry Vaughan's 'deep, but dazzling darkness', the darkness of occultism and præternaturalism, the night that is the Goddess, the 'Mother Night' of mythology, the Gnostic Night which is embodied in the Goddess Sophia, Wisdom, the night of shamanic flights. Rainer Maria Rilke in his *Duino Elegies,* wrote lyrically of this erotic night that whirls about humans and is full of angels:

> But, oh, the nights – those nights when the infinite wind
> eats at our faces! Who is immune to the night, to Night,
> ever–subtle, deceiving? Hardest of all, to the lonely,
> Night, is she gentler to lovers?[86]

Rainer Maria Rilke's poetic night is a bliss space which is clearly the external metaphor or image of the poet's inner space. It is a space of the invisible, where the Rilkean 'Open' can flourish. Novalis' night is similarly mythical:

> Downward I turn
> Toward the holy unspeakable
> Mysterious Night
> …The great wings of the spirit lift you aloft
> And fill us with joy
> Dark and unspeakable,
> Secret, as you yourself are,
> Joy that foreshadows
> A heaven to us.
> …Heavenly as flashing stars
> In each vastness
> Appear the infinite eyes
> Which the Night opens in us.[87]

Novalis, in his opening section of the *Hymns To the Night*, begins with that universal journey of heroes: into the under-world. It is a primary myth, this descent. In mythology it is often to Hell: Dante, Orpheus, Jesus, and Isis: they descend into the

---

86 R.M. Rilke: *Duino Elegies*, tr. Stephen Cohn, Carcanet Press 1989, 21
87 Novalis: *Pollen and Fragments*, 138–140

underworld. Of course, by Novalis' epoch, this nocturnal realm was identified with the inner spaces. Novalis knew that the descent into an external, mythic space was the expression of an inner, psychic descent.

When he has made the shamanic journey into the unknown, invisible, dark realm, he finds... what? His beloved, his Muse, the Queen of the Night: veritably, the Black Goddess:

> Praise the Queen of the World
> The highest messenger
> Of the holy world,
> The one who nurtures
> Holy love.
> You come, Beloved –,
> The Night is here –
> My soul is enchanted –
> The earthly day is past
> And you are mine again.
> I gaze into your deep dark eyes
> And see nothing but love and ecstasy.
> We sink upon the altar of Night
> Upon the soft bed –
> The veil drops
> And kindled by your heated touch
> The flame of the sweet offering
> Glows. (140-1)

Novalis here describes the basic story or myth of Western culture: the descent and return, the journey to fundamental ontologies, the resacralization of life, symbolized by a spiritual union expressed in erotic terms. At the heart of the *Hymnen an die Nacht* is this erotic–spiritual union, an orgasmic fusion of dualities. It is also a poetic expression of lust, of masculinist desire. For, simply, the poet goes into the Night and he makes loves to it.

In Novalis' 1800 poem, despite the Christian and theological aspects of the work, the feminine, magical dimension is continually exalted. For Novalis, the Night is a womb out of which the Son of Light, Jesus, is born; but also, our era, the Christian, is born from Mother Night. Novalis uses the typical mechanisms of shamanism – the night flight or spiritual journey – as a mythic descent and return. In section three of *Hymns To the Night* his soul soars over the world, in the typical fashion of archaic shamanism, which is the basis of all religion:

> You night raptures,
> Heavenly slumbers came over me
> The scene itself gently rose higher – my unbound, newborn
> Soul soared over the scene. The hill became a dust cloud
> and through the cloud I saw the clear features of my Beloved –
> In her eyes rested Eternity... (143)

Although he sees the mythic Night as Christian, a gathering darkness after the Light or Day of Greece, Novalis continually emphasizes the feminine, maternal aspects of this mythical Night. Novalis' Night, like Rainer Maria Rilke's, is a supremely female space: 'She bears *you* – motherly', he writes (143);

> The dark ocean's
> Blue depths
> Were a Goddess' womb.

There is much idealism in this view of a feminized soul-space, a mythic 'dreamtime' over which the Goddess presides. The upsurge of hope in the *Hymns To the Night* is very powerful:

> And into heaven's
> Infinite distance
> Filled with the lustrous world
> Into the heart of the highest spaces,
> The soul of the world withdrew
> With her powers
> To wait for the dawn
> Of new days
> And the higher destiny of the world. (150-1)

By the end of the poem, the transition is made, from the dark, maternal, feminine realm of Night to the bright, rational, masculine realm of Day or Light. 'We sink into the Father's heart', writes the poet, in the last line (159). But it is an ambiguous ending, for the new form of the feminine, the Virgin Mary, is not the erotic Black Goddess of ancient times.

Novalis describes the basic emotional displacement of the psychoanalysis of childhood: the movement of the child away from the mother towards the father; from intuition to ratiocination; from emotion to reason; from dependency to independence, from the semiotic to the symbolism realm, from femininity to masculinity; from immaturity to maturity.

Novalis simply trades in the usual poetic fare: the associations of darkness with the feminine, light with the masculine, and so on. He employs the age–old dichotomies of Western culture, where, after a night of ecstasy, the Night is renounced in favour of the Day. It is familiar rhetoric. Novalis, though, raises it to new heights because of his energy and idealism. *Hymns To the Night* is an exuberant poetic sequence, shot through and powered by flashes of inspiration and enthusiasm. It is a poem that exists all on its own. There is nothing else quite like it – not in German Romanticism, nor in poetry throughout history. It combines elements of the theological exegesis, the courtly *canso*, the philosophical tract, utopian and idealistic mysticism, and a fervent lyrical poetry.

Hymnen an die Nacht is a poem that embellishes the norms of Western culture – heterosexuality, theology, Christianity, philosophy without much developing them or questioning them. It is an uncritical poem, which restates what is already known – and felt – about Western culture. Ambiguity and doubt are not high in the poetic mix: *Hymnen an die Nacht* is a mystical poem, and about the certainty of the mystical experience. After their ecstasy, mystics feel utterly sure of their faith, their God, their duty, their life. They trust their mystical ecstasy, as one must trust one's own experiences in life. Romanticism, as we have seen, is founded on subjectivity. The Romantic poets, whether of France, Germany, Britain, America or Italy, unfailingly trust their own experiences. Indeed, artists must. Novalis' *Hymns To the Night* is constructed out of the basic, unshakeable faith in the poetic self.

᠅

Novalis continues to be read, as do Heinrich Heine, Johann Wolfgang von Goethe, both Schlegels, Friedrich Schiller and Friedrich Hölderlin. There is a richness in poets such as Goethe and Novalis that endures. Glyn Hughes writes of Novalis:

> The sustaining interest in the reading of Novalis's works is the sense of contact with a mind of visionary intensity and total commitment. The poetic achievement is in the momentary glimpses of ideal reality: what, in other contexts, we should call epiphanies. (61)

Novalis' *Hymns To the Night* articulate the rebirth at the heart of Romanticism, that self-invention which always goes to the heart of life by way of speaking of fundamental experiences – of love, death, birth and rebirth. From the womb of the Virgin Mother the shining self is reborn. Novalis' poetics, like those of Johann Wolfgang von Goethe, Friedrich Hölderlin, Heinrich Heine or Friedrich Schlegel, are those of a spiritual rebirth, a resacralization of life, a renaissance of life, in short. This is the goal of not just the Romantic poets, but of most poets throughout history.

Bibliography

M.H. Abrams: *Natural Supernaturalism: Tradition and Revolution in Romantic Literature*, Norton, New York 1971
—. ed: *English Romantic Poets: Modern Essays in Criticism*, Oxford University Press, New York 1975
Ernst Behler: *German Romantic Literary Theory*, Cambridge University Press 1993
M.B. Benn. *Hölderlin and Pindar*, The Hague, 1962
Ernst Benz: *The Mystical Sources of German Romantic Philosophy*, tr. B. Reynolds & E. Paul, Pickwick, Allison Park 1983
P. Bertaux. *Hölderlin; Essai de biographie intérieure*, Paris, 1936
—. *Le lyrisme mythique de Hölderlin*, Paris, 1936
Henri Clemens Birven: *Novalis, Magus der Romantik*, Schwab, Büdingen 1959
Richard Brinkmann, ed: *Romantik in Deutschland*, Metzler, Stuttgart 1978
Manfred Brown: *The Shape of German Romanticism*, Cornell University Press, Thaca 1979
E.M. Butler. *The Tyranny of Greece Over Germany*, Cambridge University Press, 1935
D. Constantine. *The Significance of Locality in the Poetry of Friedrich Hölderlin*, Modern Humanities Research Association, 1979
—. *Hölderlin*, Oxford University Press, 1988
S. Corngold. *Complex Pleasures: Forms of Feeling in German Literature*, Cambridge University Press, 1998
A. Del Caro. *Hölderlin: The Poetics of Being*, Wayne State University Press, 1991
Hans Eichner: *Friedrich Schlegel*, Twayne, New York 1970
Mircea Eliade: *Shamanism: Archaic Techniques of Ecstasy*, Princeton University Press, New Jersey, 1972
—. *Myths, Dreams and Mysteries*, Harper & Row, New York 1975

—. *Ordeal by Labyrinth*, University of Chicago Press 1984

R.W. Ewton: *The Literary Theory of A.W. Schlegel*, Mouthon, The Hague 1971

Richard Faber: *Novalis: die Phantasie an die Macht*, Metzler, Stuttgart 1970

Walter Feilchenfeld: *Der Einfluss Jacob Böhmes auf Novalis*, Eberia, Berlin 1922

A. Fioretos, ed. *The Solid Letter: Readings of Friedrich Hölderlin*, Stanford University Press, 1999

E. Förster, ed. *The Course of Remembrance and Other Essays on Hölderlin*, Cambridge University Press, 1997

Sara Frierichsmeyer: *The Androgyne in Early German Romanticism: Friedrich Schlegel, Novalis and the Metaphysics of Love*, Bern, New York 1983

M. Froment-Meurice. *Solitudes: From Rimbaud to Heidegger*, State University of New York Press, 1995

J.W. von Goethe. *Goethe's Faust*, tr. Louis Macniece, Faber, London, 1951

—. *Selected Poems* [with Eduard Möricke], tr. C. Middleton, University of Chicago Press, 1972

—. *Selected Poems*, ed. C. Middleton, tr. M. Hamburger et al, 1983

—. *Essays and Letters on Theory*, State University of New York Press, Albany, 1987

—. *The Sorrows of Young Werther*, Penguin, London, 1989

—. *Roman Elegies and Other Poems*, tr. M. Hamburger, Anvil Press Poetry, London, 1996

Curt Grutzmacher: *Novalis und Philippe Otto Runge*, Eidos, Munich 1964

Theodor Haering: *Novalis als Philosoph*, Kohlhammer, Stuttgart 1954

M. Hamburger. *Reason and Energy: Studies in German Literature*, Weidenfeld & Nicolson, 1970

—. *Testimonies: Selected Shorter Prose, 1950-1987*, Carcanet, 1989

—. *The Truth of Poetry*, Anvil Press Poetry, 1996

Bruce Haywood: *The Veil of Imagery: A Study of the Poetic Works of Friedrich von Hardenburg*, Harvard University Press, Cambridge, Mass., 1959

Frederick Heibel: *Novalis: German Poet, European Thinker, Christian Mystic*, AMS, New York 1969

Heinrich Heine: *The Complete Poems of Heinrich Heine*, tr. Hal Draper, Suhrkamp/ Insel, Boston 1982

– *The North Sea*, tr. Vernon Watkins, Faber 1955

Friedrich Hölderlin. *Complete Works*, ed. N. von Hellingrath *et al*, Berlin, 1923

—. *Hölderlin Sämtliche Werke*, Große Stuttgarter Ausgabe, Stuttgart, 1943-77

—. *Selected Poems*, tr. J.B. Leishman, Hogarth Press, 1954

—. *Hymns and Fragments*, tr. R. Siebruth, Princeton University Press, 1984

—. *Hölderlin Folioheft*, ed. D.E. Sattler & E.,E. George, Frankfurt, 1986
—. *Hyperion and Selected Poems*, ed. E.L. Santer, Continuum, 1992
—. *Poems and Fragments*, tr. M. Hamburger, Anvil Press, 1994
—. *Selected Poems and Fragments*, tr. M. Hamburger, Penguin, 1998
—. *Hölderlin's Songs of Light*, tr. M. Hamburger, ed. J.M. Robinson, Crescent Moon, 2012
Glyn Tegai Hughes: *Romantic German Literature*, Edward Arnold, 1979
L. Kempter. *Hölderlin und die Mythologie*, Zurich, 1929
D.F. Krell. "Nietzsche Hölderlin Empedocles", *Graduate Faculty Philosophy Journal*, 15, 2, 1991
—. *Lunar Voices: Of Tragedy, Poetry, Fiction, and Thought*, Chicago University Press, 1995
—. *The Recalcitrant Art: Diotima's Letters to Hölderlin and Related Missives*, State University of New York Press, Albany, 2000
Alice Kuzniar: *Delayed Endings: Nonclosure in Novalis and Hölderlin*, University of Georgia Press, Athens 1987
Weston La Barre: *The Ghost Dance*, Allen & Unwin 1972
Philippe Lacoue-Labarthe & Jean-Luc Nancy, eds: *The Literary Absolute: The Theory of Literature in German Romanticism*, State University of New York Press, Albany 1988
G. Lemout. *The Poet as Thinker: Hölderlin in France*, Camden House, 1994
E.C. Mason. *Hölderlin and Goethe*, P. Lang, 1975
Géza von Molnar: *Novalis's Fichte Studies*, Mouton, The Hague 1970
—. *Romantic Vision, Ethical Context: Novalis and Artistic Autonomy*, University of Minnesota Press, Minneapolis 1987
E. Meister. *Prosa, 1931 bis 1979*, Heidelberg, 1989
C. Middleton. *The Poet's Vocation: Letters of Hölderlin, Rimbaud and Hart Crane*, Austin, Texas, c. 1967
M. Montgomery. *Friedrich Hölderlin and the German Neo-Hellenic Movement*, London, 1923
Bruno Müller: *Novalis – der dichter als Mittler*, Lang, Bern 1984
John Neubauer: *Bifocal Vision: Novalis's Philosophy of Nature and Disease*, Chapel Hill 1972
Novalis: *Pollen and Fragments: Selected Poetry and Prose*, tr. Arthur Versluis, Phanes Press, Grand Rapids, 1989
—*Hymns To the Night and Other Selected Writings*, tr. Charles E. Passage, Bobbs-Merrill Company, Indianapolis 1960
—. *Hymns To the Night*, Crescent Moon, 2010
Novalis Schriften. Die Werke Friedrichs von Hardenberg, ed. Richard Samuel, Hans–Joachim Mähl & Gerhard Schulz, Kohlhammer, Stuttgart 1960–88
K.J. Obenauer. *Hölderlin-Novalis*, Jena, 1925
S.S. Pawer: *Heine: Buch der Lieder*, Arnold 1960
—. *Heine, the Tragic Satirist: A Study of the Later Poetry 1827–56*,

Cambridge University Press 1961

—. *Heine's Jewish Comedy: A Study of His Portraits of Jews and Judaism*, Clarnedon Press 1983

—. *Frankenstein's Island: England and the English in the Writings of Heinrich Heine*, Cambridge University Press 1986

R. Peacock. *Hölderlin*, Methuen, 1973

A. Pellegrini. *Friedrich Hölderlin*, Walter de Gruter, Berlin, 1965

Ritchie Robertson: *Heine*, Peter Halban, 1988

L.S. Salzberger. *Hölderlin*, Cambridge University Press, 1952

E.L. Santer. *Friedrich Hölderlin: Narrative Vigilance and the Poetic Imagination*, New Brunswick, 1986

Nicholas Saul: *History and Poetry in Novalis and in the Tradition of the German Enlightenment*, Institute of Germanic Studies, 1984

Helmut Schanze: *Romantik und Aufklärung, Unterschungen zu Friedrich Schlegel und Novalis*, Carl, Nürnberg 1966

—ed. *Friedrich Schlegel und die Kunstheorie Seiner Zeit*, Wissenschaftliche Buchgesellschaft, Darmstadt 1985

A.W. Schlegel: *Kritische Ausgabe der Verlesungen*, ed. Ernst Behler & Frank Jolles, Schöningen, Paderborn, 1989–

F. Schlegel: *Gespräch über die Poesie, Kritische Friedrich Schlegel Ausgabe*, Schöningh, Paderborn, 1958–

—. *Lucinde and the Fragments*, tr. Peter Firchow, University of Minnesota Press, Minneapolis 1971

A. Seyhan. *Representation and its Discontents: The Critical Legacy of German Romanticism*, University of California Press, Berkeley, 1992

E. Sewell. *The Orphic Voice: Poetry and Natural History*, Routledge, 1961

D. Simpson *et al*, eds. *German Aesthetic and Literary Criticism*, Cambridge University Press, 3 vols, 1984-85

E.L. Stahl. *Hölderlin's Symbolism*, Oxford University Press, 1945

A. Stansfield. *Hölderlin*, Manchester University Press, 1944

P. Szondi. *Hölderlin–Studien*, Insel, Frankfurt, 1967

Ronald Taylor: *The Romantic Tradition in Germany*, Methuen 1970

Ralph Tymms: *German Romanticism*, Methuen 1955

R. Ungar. *Hölderlin's Major Poetry*, Indiana University Press, Bloomington, 1975

—. *Friedrich Hölderlin*, Twayne, 1984

A. Warminksi. *Readings in Interpretation: Hölderlin, Hegel, Heidegger*, University of Minnesota Press, Minneapolis, 1987

K. Wheeler, ed. *German Aesthetic and Literary Criticism, The Romantic Ironists and Goethe*, Cambridge University Press, 1984

Illustrations

Johann Wolfgang von Goethe

Heinrich Heine

Heinrich Heine

Friedrich Hölderlin

Friedrich Hölderlin

Novalis

Novalis

Sophie von Kühn

Karl Wilhelm Friedrich Schlegel

SELECTED WORKS

FRIEDRICH HÖLDERLIN

HYPERONS SCHIKSAALSLIED

Ihr wandelt droben im Licht
  Auf weichen Boden, seelige Genien!
    Glänzende Götterlüfte
      Rühren euch leicht,
        Wie die Finger der Künstlerin
          Heilige Saiten.

Schiksaallos, wie der schlafende
  Säugling, athmen die Himmlischen;
    Keusch bewahrt
      In bescheidener Knospe,
        Blühet ewig
          Ihnen der Geist,
            Und die seeligen Augen
              Bliken in stiller
                Ewiger Klarheit.

Doch uns ist gegeben,
  Auf keiner Stätte zu ruhn,
    Es schwinden, es fallen
      Die leidenden Menschen
        Blindlings von einer
          Stunde zur andern,
            Wie Wasser von Lippe
              Zu Lippe geworfen,
                Jahr lang ins Ungewisse hinab.

HYPERION'S SONG OF FATE

You walk above in the light,
　Weightless tread a soft floor, blessed genii!
　　Radiant the gods' mild breezes
　　　Gently play on you
　　　　As the girl artist's fingers
　　　　　On holy strings.

Fateless the Heavenly breathe
　Like an unweaned infant asleep;
　　Chastely preserved
　　　In modest bud
　　　　For ever their minds
　　　　　Are in flower
　　　　　　And their blissful eyes
　　　　　　　Eternally tranquil gaze,
　　　　　　　　Eternally clear.

But we are fated
　To find no foothold, no rest,
　　And suffering mortals
　　　Dwindle and fall
　　　　Headlong from one
　　　　　Hour to the next,
　　　　　　Hurled like water
　　　　　　　From ledge to ledge
　　　　　　　　Downward for years to the vague abyss.[1]

1 Friedrich Hölderlin's poetry's translated by Michael Hamburger. From *Hölderlin's Songs of Light*, ed. J.M. Robinson, Crescent Moon, 2012.

AN DIOTIMA

Schönes Leben! du lebst, wie die zarten Blüthen im Winter,
  In der gealterten Welt blühst du verschlossen, allein.
Liebend strebst du hinaus, dich zu sonnen am Lichte des
                                          Frühlings,
  Zu erwarmen an ihr suchst du die Jugend der Welt.
Deine Sonne, die schönere Zeit, ist untergegangen
  Und in frostiger Nacht zanken Orkane sich nun.

TO DIOTIMA

Beautiful being, you live as do delicate blossoms in winter,
  In a world that's grown old hidden you blossom, alone.
Lovingly outward you press to bask in the light of the
                                  springtime,
  To be warmed by it still, look for the youth of the world.
But your sun, the lovelier world, has gone down now,
  And the quarrelling gales rage in an icy bleak night.

UNTER DEN ALPEN GESUNGEN

Heilige Unschuld, du der Menschen und der
Götter liebste vertrauteste! du magst im
Hauße oder draußen ihnen zu Füßen
           Sizen, den Alten,

Immerzufriedner Weisheit voll; denn manches
Gute kennet der Mann, doch staunet er, dem
Wild gleich, oft zum Himmel, aber wie rein ist
           Reine, dir alles!

Siehe! das rauhe Thier des Feldes, gerne
Dient und trauet es dir, der stumme Wald spricht
Wie von Alters, seine Sprüche zu dir, es
           Lehren die Berge

Heil'ge Geseze dich, und was nocht jezt uns
Vielerfahrenen offenbar der große
Vater werden heißt, du darfst es allein uns
           Helle verkünden.

So mit den Himmlischen allein zu seyn, und
Geht vorüber das Licht, und Strom und Wind, und
Zeit eilt hin zum Ort, vor ihnen ein stetes
           Auge zu haben,

Seeliger weiß und wünsch' ich nichts, so lange
Nicht auch mich, wie die Weide, fort die Fluth nimmt,
Daß wohl aufgehoben, schlafend dahin ich
           Muß in den Woogen;

SUNG BENEATH THE ALPS

Innocence, you the holy, dearest and nearest
Both to men and to gods! In the house or
Out of doors alike to sit at the ancients'
                    Feet it behoves you,

Ever contented wisdom yours; for men know
Much that's good, yet like animals often
Scan the heavens perplexed; to you, though, how pure are
                    All things, you pure one!

Look, the rough grassland beast is glad to serve and
Trust you; mute though it be, yet the forest
Now as ever yields its oracles up, the
                    Mountains still teach you

God-hallowed laws, and that which even now the
Mighty Father desires to make known to
Us the much experienced, you, and you only
                    Clearly may tell us.

Being alone with heavenly powers, and when the
Light begins to pass by, and swiftly river,
Wind and time seek out the place, with a constant
                    Eye then to face them –

Nothing more blessed I know, nor want, as long as
Not like willows me too the flood sweeps on, and
Well looked after, sleeping, down I must travel,
                    Waves for my bedding;

Aber es bleibt daheim gern, wer in treuem
Busen Göttliches hält, und frei will ich, so
Lang ich darf, euch all', ihr Sprachen des Himmels!
Deuten und singen.

Gladly, though, he will stay at home who harbours
Things divine in his heart; and you, all Heaven's
Languages, freely, as long as I may, I'll
                    Sing and interpret.

IHRE GENESUNG

Sich! dein Liebstes, Natur, leidet und shläft und du
  Allesheilende, säumst? oder ihr seids nicht mehr,
    Zarte Lüfte des Aethers,
      Und ihr Quellen des Morgenlichts?

Alle Blumen der Erd, alle die goldenen
  Frohen Früchte des hains, alle sie heilen nicht
    Dieses Leben, ihr Götter,
      Das ihr selber doch euch erzogt?

Ach! schon athmet und tönt heilige Lebenslust
  Ihr im reizenden Wort wieder, wie sonst und schon
    Glänzt in zärtlicher Jugend
      Deine Blume, wie sonst, dich an,

Heilige Natur, o du, welche zu oft, zu oft,
  Wenn ich trauernd versank, lächelnd das sweifelnde
    Haupt mit Gaaben umkränzte,
      Jugendliche, nun auch, wie sonst!

Wenn ich altre dereinst, siehe so geb ich dir,
  Die mich täglich verjüngt, Allesverwandelnde,
    Deiner Flamme die Schlaken,
      Und ein anderer leb ich auf.

HER RECOVERY

Nature, look, your most loved drowses and ails, and you
    Dally, healer of all? Have you grown weak, then, tired,
        Gentle breezes of Aether,
            Limpid sources of morning light?

All the flowers of the earth, all the deep golden-hued
    Happy fruits of the grove, how can it be that all
        Fail to cure this one life which,
            Gods, you raised for your own delight?

Ah, already restored, holy desire to live
    Breathes and sounds in her talk, charming as ever, and
        Tenderly youthful your darling
            Gleams at you as she did before,

Holy Nature, the same who all too often when
    Sadness made me sink down, smiling would garland my
        Head with gifts, with your riches,
            Youthful Nature, now too restored!

Look, one day when I'm old, you that transmute all things
    And now daily renew youth in me, I will give
        To your flame the dead cinders
            And revive as a different man.

"GEH UNTER, SCHÖNE SONNE"

Geh unter, schöne Sonne, sie achteten
  Nur wenig dein, sie kannten dich, Heilg, nicht,
    Denn mühelos und stille bist du
      Über den mühsamen aufgegangen.

Mir gehst du freundlich unter und auf, o Licht!
  Und wohl erkennt mein Auge dich, herrliches!
    Denn göttlich stille ehren lernt' ich
      Da Diotima den Sinn mir heilte.

O du desHimmels Botin! wie lauscht ich dir!
  Dir, Diotima! Liebe! wie sah von dir
    Zum goldnen Tage dieses Auge
      Glänzend und dankend empor. Da rauschten

Lebendiger die Quellen, es athmeten
  Der dunkeln Erde Blüthen mich liebend an,
    Und lächelnd über Silberwolken
      Neigte sich seegnend herab der Aether.

"GO DOWN, THEN, LOVELY SUN"

Go down, then, lovely sun, for but little they
    Regarded you, nor, holy one, knew your worth,
        Since without toil you rose, and quiet,
            Over a people for ever toiling.

To me, however, kindly you rise and set,
    O glorious light, and brightly my eyes respond,
        For godly, silent reverence I
            Learned when Diotima soothed my frenzy.

O how I listened, Heaven's own messenger,
    To you, my teacher! Love! How to the golden day
        These eyes transfused with thanks looked up from
            Gazing at you. And at once more living

The brooks began to murmur, more lovingly
    The blossoms of dark Earth breathed their scent at me
        And through the silver clouds a smiling
            Aether bowed down to bestow his blessing.

HEINRICH HEINE

THE SEA HATH ITS PEARLS

The sea hath its pearls,
The heaven hath its stars;
But my heart, my heart,
My heart hath its love.

Great are the sea, and the heaven;
Yet greater is my heart,
And fairer than pearls or stars
Flashes and beams my love.

Thou little, youthful maiden,
Come unto my great heart;
My heart, and the sea and the heaven
Are melting away with love![2]

---

2 Translated by Henry Wadsworth Longfellow (1807-1882).

E'EN AS A LOVELY FLOWER

E'en as a lovely flower,
So fair, so pure thou art;
I gaze on thee, and sadness
Comes stealing o'er my heart.

My hands I fain had folded
Upon thy soft brown hair,
Praying that God may keep thee
So lovely, pure and fair.[3]

3 Translated by Kate Freiligrath Kroeker (1845-1904).

THIS MAD CARNIVAL OF LOVING

This mad carnival of loving,
This wild orgy of the flesh,
Ends at last and we two, sobered,
Look at one another, yawning.

Emptied the inflaming cup
That was filled with sensuous potions,
Foaming, almost running over –
Emptied is the flaming cup.

All the violins are silent
That impelled our feet to dancing,
To the giddy dance of passion –
Silent are the violins.

All the lanterns now are darkened
That once poured their streaming brilliance
On the masquerades and murmurs –
Darkened now are all the lanterns.[4]

---

4 Translated by Louis Untermeyer, in *Poetica Erotica*, ed. T.R. Smith. New York: Crown Publishers, 1921.

I LOVE THIS WHITE AND SLENDER BODY

Love this white and slender body,
These limbs that answer Love's caresses,
Passionate eyes, and forehead covered
With heavy waves of thick, black tresses.

You are the very one I've searched for
In many lands, in every weather.
You are my sort; you understand me;
As equals we can talk together.

In me you've found the man you care for.
And, for a while, you'll richly pay me
With kindness, kisses and endearments –
And then, as usual, you'll betray me.[5]

---

[5] Translated by Louis Untermeyer, in *Poetica Erotica*, ed. T.R. Smith. New York: Crown Publishers, 1921.

THE OLD DREAM COMES AGAIN TO ME

The old dream comes again to me:
With May-night stars above,
We two sat under the linden-tree
And swore eternal love.

Again and again we plighted troth,
We chattered, and laughed, and kissed;
To make me well remember my oath
You gave me a bite on the wrist.

O darling with the eyes serene,
And with the teeth so white!
The vows were proper to the scene,
Superfluous was the bite.[6]

---

6 Translated by James Thomson (1834-1882)

WHY THE ROSES ARE SO PALE

Dearest, canst thou tell me why
The rose should be so pale?
And why the azure violet
Should wither in the vale?

And why the lark should in the cloud
So sorrowfully sing?
And why from loveliest balsam-buds
A scent of death should spring?

And why the sun upon the mead
So chillingly should frown?
And why the earth should, like a grave,
Be moldering and brown?

And why it is that I myself
So languishing should be?
And why it is, my heart of hearts,
That thou forsakest me?[7]

---

7 Translated by Richard Garnett (1835-1906).

NOVALIS

From *HYMNS TO THE NIGHT*

4

Nun weiß ich, wenn der letzte Morgen sein wird – wenn das
Licht nicht mehr die Nacht und die Liebe scheucht – wenn der
Schlummer ewig und nur Ein unerschöpflicher Traum sein
wird. Himmlische Müdigkeit fühl ich in mir. – Weit und
ermüdend ward mir die Wallfahrt zum heiligen Grabe,
drückend das Kreuz. Die kristallene Woge, die gemeinen
Sinnen unvernehmlich, in des Hügels dunkelm Schoß quillt, an
dessen Fuß die irdische Flut bricht, wer sie gekostet, wer oben
stand auf dem Grenzgebürge der Welt, und hinübersah in das
neue Land, in der Nacht Wohnsitz – wahrlich der kehrt nicht in
das Treiben der Welt zurück, in das Land, wo das Licht in
ewiger Unruh hauset.
Oben baut er sich Hütten, Hütten des Friedens, sehnt sich und
liebt, schaut hinüber, bis die willkommenste aller Stunden
hinunter ihn in den Brunnen der Quelle zieht – das Irdische
schwimmt obenauf, wird von Stürmen zurückgeführt, aber was
heilig durch der Liebe Berührung ward, rinnt aufgelöst in
verborgenen Gängen auf das jenseitige Gebiet, wo es, wie
Düfte, sich mit entschlummerten Lieben mischt. Noch weckst
du, muntres Licht den Müden zur Arbeit – flößest fröhliches
Leben mir ein – aber du lockst mich von der Erinnerung
moosigem Denkmal nicht. Gern will ich die fleißigen Hände
rühren, überall umschaun, wo du mich brauchst – rühmen
deines Glanzes volle Pracht – unverdrossen verfolgen deines
künstlichen Werks schönen Zusammenhang – gern betrachten
deiner gewaltigen, leuchtenden Uhr sinnvollen Gang –
ergründen der Kräfte Ebenmaß und die Regeln des
Wunderspiels unzähliger Räume und ihrer Zeiten. Aber getreu
der Nacht bleibt mein geheimes Herz, und der schaffenden

Liebe, ihrer Tochter. Kannst du mir zeigen ein ewig treues
Herz? hat deine Sonne freundliche Augen, die mich erkennen?
fassen deine Sterne meine verlangende Hand? Geben mir
wieder den zärtlichen Druck und das kosende Wort? Hast du
mit Farben und leichtem Umriß Sie geziert – oder war Sie es,
die deinem Schmuck höhere, liebere Bedeutung gab? Welche
Wollust, welchen Genuß bietet dein Leben, die aufwögen des
Todes Entzückungen? Trägt nicht alles, was uns begeistert, die
Farbe der Nacht? Sie trägt dich mütterlich und ihr verdankst du
all deine Herrlichkeit. Du verflögst in dir selbst – in endlosen
Raum zergingst du, wenn sie dich nicht hielte, dich nicht
bände, daß du warm würdest und flammend die Welt zeugtest.
Wahrlich ich war, eh du warst – die Mutter schickte mit meinen
Geschwistern mich, zu bewohnen deine Welt, sie zu heiligen
mit Liebe, daß sie ein ewig angeschautes Denkmal werde – zu
bepflanzen sie mit unverwelklichen Blumen. Noch reiften sie
nicht diese göttlichen Gedanken – Noch sind der Spuren
unserer Offenbarung wenig – Einst zeigt deine Uhr das Ende
der Zeit, wenn du wirst wie unsereiner, und voll Sehnsucht
und Inbrunst auslöschest und stirbst. In mir fühl ich deiner
Geschäftigkeit Ende – himmlische Freiheit, selige Rückkehr. In
wilden Schmerzen erkenn ich deine Entfernung von unsrer
Heimat, deinen Widerstand gegen den alten, herrlichen
Himmel. Deine Wut und dein Toben ist vergebens.
Unverbrennlich steht das Kreuz – eine Siegesfahne unsers
Geschlechts.

Hinüber wall ich,
Und jede Pein
Wird einst ein Stachel
Der Wollust sein.
Noch wenig Zeiten,
So bin ich los,
Und liege trunken
Der Lieb im Schoß.
Unendliches Leben
Wogt mächtig in mir
Ich schaue von oben
Herunter nach dir.
An jenem Hügel
Verlischt dein Glanz –
Ein Schatten bringet
Den kühlenden Kranz.
O! sauge, Geliebter,
Gewaltig mich an,
Daß ich entschlummern
Und lieben kann.
Ich fühle des Todes
Verjüngende Flut,
Zu Balsam und Äther
Verwandelt mein Blut –
Ich lebe bei Tage
Voll Glauben und Mut
Und sterbe die Nächte
In heiliger Glut.

4

Now I know when will come the last morning: when the Light no more scares away the Night and Love, when sleep shall be without waking, and but one continuous dream. I feel in me a celestial exhaustion. Long and weariful was my pilgrimage to the holy grave, and crushing was the cross. The crystal wave, which, imperceptible to the ordinary sense, springs in the dark bosom of the mound against whose foot breaks the flood of the world, he who has tasted it, he who has stood on the mountain frontier of the world, and looked across into the new land, into the abode of the Night, verily he turns not again into the tumult of the world, into the land where dwells the Light in ceaseless unrest. On those heights he builds for himself tabernacles – tabernacles of peace; there longs and loves and gazes across, until the welcomest of all hours draws him down into the waters of the spring. Afloat above remains what is earthly, and is swept back in storms; but what became holy by the touch of Love, runs free through hidden ways to the region beyond, where, like odours, it mingles with love asleep. Still wakest thou, cheerful Light, that weary man to his labour, and into me pourest gladsome life; but thou wilest me not away from Memory's moss-grown monument. Gladly will I stir busy hands, everywhere behold where thou hast need of me; bepraise the rich pomp of thy splendor; pursue unwearied the lovely harmonies of thy skilled handicraft; gladly contemplate the clever pace of thy mighty, radiant clock; explore the balance of the forces and the laws of the wondrous play of countless worlds and their seasons; but true to the Night remains my secret heart, and to creative Love, her daughter. Canst *thou* show me a heart eternally true? Has thy sun friendly eyes that know me? Do thy stars lay hold of my longing hand? Do they return me the tender pressure and the caressing word? Was it thou did bedeck them with colours and a flickering outline? Or was it *she* who gave to thy jewels a higher, a dearer significance? What delight, what pleasure offers *thy* life, to outweigh the transports of Death? Wears not everything that inspirits us the livery of the Night? Thy mother, it is she brings thee forth, and to her thou owest all thy glory. Thou wouldst vanish into thyself, thou wouldst dissipate in boundless space, if she did not hold thee fast, if she swaddled thee not, so that thou grewest warm, and flaming, gavest birth to the universe. Verily I was before thou wast; the mother sent me with sisters to inhabit thy world, to sanctify it with love that it might be an ever-present memorial, to plant it with flowers unfading. As yet they have not ripened, these thoughts divine; as yet is there small trace of our coming apocalypse. One day thy clock will point to the end of Time, and then thou shalt be as one of us, and shalt, full of ardent longing, be extinguished and die. I feel in me the close of thy activity, I taste heavenly freedom, and happy restoration. With wild pangs I recognize thy distance from our home, thy feud with the ancient, glorious Heaven. Thy rage and thy raving are in vain. Inconsumable stands the cross, victory-flag of our race.[8]

8 The translation of *Hymns To the Night* is by George MacDonald, from *Hymns To the Night*, Crescent Moon, 2012.

Over I pilgrim
Where every pain
Zest only of pleasure
Shall one day remain.
Yet a few moments
Then free am I,
And intoxicated
In Love's lap lie.
Life everlasting
Lifts, wave-like, at me:
I gaze from its summit
Down after thee.
Oh Sun, thou must vanish
Yon yon hillock beneath;
A shadow will bring thee
Thy cooling wreath.
Oh draw at my heart, love,
Draw till I'm gone,
That, fallen asleep, I
Still may love on.
I feel the flow of
Death's youth-giving flood;
To balsam and æther, it
Changes my blood!
I live all the daytime
In faith and in might:
And in holy rapture
I die every night.

Sehnsucht nach dem Tode
Hinunter in der Erde Schoß,
Weg aus des Lichtes Reichen,
Der Schmerzen Wut und wilder Stoß
Ist froher Abfahrt Zeichen.
Wir kommen in dem engen Kahn
Geschwind am Himmelsufer an.
Gelobt sei uns die ewge Nacht,
Gelobt der ewge Schlummer.
Wohl hat der Tag uns warm gemacht,
Und welk der lange Kummer.
Die Lust der Fremde ging uns aus,
Zum Vater wollen wir nach Haus.
Was sollen wir auf dieser Welt
Mit unsrer Lieb und Treue.
Das Alte wird hintangestellt,
Was soll uns dann das Neue.
O! einsam steht und tiefbetrübt,
Wer heiß und fromm die Vorzeit liebt.
Die Vorzeit wo die Sinne licht
In hohen Flammen brannten,
Des Vaters Hand und Angesicht
Die Menschen noch erkannten.
Und hohen Sinns, einfältiglich
Noch mancher seinem Urbild glich.
Die Vorzeit, wo noch blütenreich
Uralte Stämme prangten,
Und Kinder für das Himmelreich
Nach Qual und Tod verlangten.
Und wenn auch Lust und Leben sprach
Doch manches Herz für Liebe brach.

Die Vorzeit, wo in Jugendglut
Gott selbst sich kundgegeben
Und frühem Tod in Liebesmut
Geweiht sein süßes Leben.
Und Angst und Schmerz nicht von sich trieb,
Damit er uns nur teuer blieb.
Mit banger Sehnsucht sehn wir sie
In dunkle Nacht gehüllet,
In dieser Zeitlichkeit wird nie
Der heiße Durst gestillet.
Wir müssen nach der Heimat gehn,
Um diese heilge Zeit zu sehn.
Was hält noch unsre Rückkehr auf,
Die Liebsten ruhn schon lange.
Ihr Grab schließt unsern Lebenslauf,
Nun wird uns weh und bange.
Zu suchen haben wir nichts mehr –
Das Herz ist satt – die Welt ist leer.
Unendlich und geheimnisvoll
Durchströmt uns süßer Schauer –
Mir däucht, aus tiefen Fernen scholl
Ein Echo unsrer Trauer.
Die Lieben sehnen sich wohl auch
Und sandten uns der Sehnsucht Hauch.
Hinunter zu der süßen Braut,
Zu Jesus, dem Geliebten –
Getrost, die Abenddämmrung graut
Den Liebenden, Betrübten.
Ein Traum bricht unsre Banden los
Und senkt uns in des Vaters Schoß.

6

Longing for Death
Into the bosom of the earth!
Out of the Light's dominions!
Death's pains are but the bursting forth
Of glad departures pinions!
Swift in the narrow little boat,
Swift to the heavenly shore we float!
Blest be the everlasting Night,
And blest the endless slumber!
We are heated with the day too bright,
And withered up with cumber!
We're weary of that life abroad:
Come, we will now go home to God!
Why longer in this world abide?
Why love and truth here cherish?
That which is old is set aside –
For us the new may perish!
Alone he stands and sore downcast
Who loves with pious warmth the Past.
The Past where yet the human spirit
In lofty flames did rise;
Where men the Father did inherit,
His countenance recognize;
And, in simplicity made ripe,
Many grew like their archetype.
The Past wherein, still rich in bloom
Old stems did burgeon glorious;
And children, for the world to come,
Sought pain and death victorious;
And, through both life and pleasure spake,
Yet many a heart for love did break.

The Past, where to the flow of youth
God yet himself declared;
And early death in loving truth
The young beheld, and dared –
Anguish and torture parient bore
To prove they loved him as of yore
With anxious yearning now we see
That Past in darkness drenched;
With this world's water never we
Shall find our hot thirst quenched:
To our old home we have to go
That blessed time again to know.
What yet doth hinder our return?
Long since repose our precious!
Their grave is of our life the bourne;
We shrink from times ungracious!
By not a hope are we decoyed:
The heart is full; the world is void.
Infinite and mysterious,
Thrills through me a sweet trembling,
As if from far there echoed thus
A sigh, our grief resembling:
The dear ones long as well as I,
And sent to me their waiting sigh.
Down to the sweet bride, and away
To the beloved Jesus!
Courage! the evening shades grow gray,
Of all our griefs to ease us!
A dream will dash our chains apart,
And lay us on the Father's heart.

JOHANN WOLFGANG VON GOETHE

MAY SONG

How fair doth Nature
Appear again!
How bright the sunbeams!
How smiles the plain!
The flowers are bursting
From every bough,
And thousand voices
Each bush yields now.
And joy and gladness
Fill every breast!
Oh earth! – oh sunlight!
Oh rapture blest!
Oh love! oh loved one!
As golden bright,
As clouds of morning
On yonder height!
Thou blessest gladly
The smiling field, –
The world in fragrant
Vapour concealed.
Oh maiden, maiden,
How love I thee!
Thine eye, how gleams it!
How lovest thou me!
The blithe lark loveth
Sweet song and air,
The morning floweret
Heaven's incense fair,
As I now love thee
With fond desire,
For thou dost give me

Youth, joy, and fire,
For new-born dances
And minstrelsy.
Be ever happy,
As thou lovest me!

1775[9]

9 Poems by Goethe are translated by Edgar Alfred Bowring, 1853.

THE MUSES' SON

Through field and wood to stray,
And pipe my tuneful lay, –
'Tis thus my days are pass'd;
And all keep tune with me,
And move in harmony,
And so on, to the last.
To wait I scarce have power
The garden's earliest flower,
The tree's first bloom in Spring;
They hail my joyous strain, –
When Winter comes again,
Of that sweet dream I sing.
My song sounds far and near,
O'er ice it echoes clear,
Then Winter blossoms bright;
And when his blossoms fly,
Fresh raptures meet mine eye,
Upon the well-till'd height.
When 'neath the linden tree,
Young folks I chance to see,
I set them moving soon;
His nose the dull lad curls,
The formal maiden whirls,
Obedient to my tune.
Wings to the feet ye lend,
O'er hill and vale ye send
The lover far from home;
When shall I, on your breast,.
Ye kindly muses, rest,
And cease at length to roam?
                    1800

THE BEAUTIFUL NIGHT

Now I leave this cottage lowly,
Where my love hath made her home,
And with silent footstep slowly
Through the darksome forest roam,
Luna breaks through oaks and bushes,
Zephyr hastes her steps to meet,
And the waving birch-tree blushes,
Scattering round her incense sweet.
Grateful are the cooling breezes
Of this beauteous summer night,
Here is felt the charm that pleases,
And that gives the soul delight.
Boundless is my joy; yet, Heaven,
Willingly I'd leave to thee
Thousand such nights, were one given
By my maiden loved to me!

1767-8

HAPPINESS AND VISION

Together at the altar we
In vision oft were seen by thee,
Thyself as bride, as bridegroom I.
Oft from thy mouth full many a kiss
In an unguarded hour of bliss
I then would steal, while none were by.
The purest rapture we then knew,
The joy those happy hours gave too,
When tasted, fled, as time fleets on.
What now avails my joy to me?
Like dreams the warmest kisses flee,
Like kisses, soon all joys are gone.

1767-8

RESTLESS LOVE

Through rain, through snow,
Through tempest go!
'Mongst streaming caves,
O'er misty waves,
On, on! still on!
Peace, rest have flown!
Sooner through sadness
I'd wish to be slain,
Than all the gladness
Of life to sustain
All the fond yearning
That heart feels for heart,
Only seems burning
To make them both smart.
How shall I fly?
Forestwards hie?
Vain were all strife!
Bright crown of life.
Turbulent bliss, –
Love, thou art this!

1789

LOVE AS A LANDSCAPE PAINTER

On a rocky peak once sat I early,
Gazing on the mist with eyes unmoving;
Stretch'd out like a pall of greyish texture,
All things round, and all above it cover'd.
Suddenly a boy appear'd beside me,
Saying "Friend, what meanest thou by gazing
On the vacant pall with such composure?
Hast thou lost for evermore all pleasure
Both in painting cunningly, and forming?"
On the child I gazed, and thought in secret:
"Would the boy pretend to be a master?"
"Wouldst thou be for ever dull and idle,"
Said the boy, "no wisdom thou'lt attain to;
See, I'll straightway paint for thee a figure, –
How to paint a beauteous figure, show thee."
And he then extended his fore-finger, –
(Ruddy was it as a youthful rosebud)
Toward the broad and far outstretching carpet,
And began to draw there with his finger.
First on high a radiant sun he painted,
Which upon mine eyes with splendour glistened,
And he made the clouds with golden border,
Through the clouds he let the sunbeams enter;
Painted then the soft and feathery summits
Of the fresh and quickened trees, behind them
One by one with freedom drew the mountains;
Underneath he left no lack of water,
But the river painted so like Nature,
That it seemed to glitter in the sunbeams,
That it seemed against its banks to murmur.

Ah, there blossomed flowers beside the river,
And bright colours gleamed upon the meadow,
Gold, and green, and purple, and enamelled,
All like carbuncles and emeralds seeming!
Bright and clear he added then the heavens,
And the blue-tinged mountains far and farther,
So that I, as though newborn, enraptured
Gazed on, now the painter, now the picture.
Then spake he: "Although I have convinced thee
That this art I understand full surely,
Yet the hardest still is left to show thee."
Thereupon he traced, with pointed finger,
And with anxious care, upon the forest,
At the utmost verge, where the strong sunbeams
From the shining ground appeared reflected,
Traced the figure of a lovely maiden,
Fair in form, and clad in graceful fashion,
Fresh the cheeks beneath her brown locks' ambush,
And the cheeks possessed the selfsame colour
As the finger that had served to paint them.
"Oh thou boy!" exclaimed I then, "what master
In his school received thee as his pupil,
Teaching thee so truthfully and quickly
Wisely to begin, and well to finish?"
Whilst I still was speaking, lo, a zephyr
Softly rose, and set the tree-tops moving,
Curling all the wavelets on the river,
And the perfect maiden's veil, too, filled it,
And to make my wonderment still greater,
Soon the maiden set her foot in motion.
On she came, approaching toward the station
Where still sat I with my arch instructor.
As now all, yes, all thus moved together, –
Flowers, river, trees, the veil, – all moving, –
And the gentle foot of that most fair one,

Can ye think that on my rock I lingered,
Like a rock, as though fast-chained and silent?

1788

THE BLISS OF ABSENCE

Drink, oh youth, joy's purest ray
From thy loved one's eyes all day,
And her image paint at night!
Better rule no lover knows,
Yet true rapture greater grows,
When far severed from her sight.
Powers eternal, distance, time,
Like the might of stars sublime,
Gently rock the blood to rest,
Over my senses softness steals,
Yet my bosom lighter feels,
And I daily am more blest.
Though I can forget her never,
Yet my mind is free from care,
I can calmly live and move;
Unperceived infatuation
Longing turns to adoration,
Turns to reverence my love.
Never can cloud, however light,
Float in ether's regions bright,
When drawn upwards by the sun,
As my heart in rapturous calm.
Free from envy and alarm,
Ever love I her alone!

1767-9

PRESENCE

All things give token of thee!
As soon as the bright sun is shining,
Thou too wilt follow, I trust.
When in the garden thou walkest,
Thou then art the rose of all roses,
Lily of lilies as well.
When thou dost move in the dance,
Then each constellation moves also;
With thee and round thee they move.
Night! oh, what bliss were the night!
For then thou overshadowest the lustre,
Dazzling and fair, of the moon.
Dazzling and beauteous art thou,
And flowers, and moon, and the planets
Homage pay, Sun, but to thee.
Sun! to me also be thou
Creator of days bright and glorious;
Life and Eternity this!

1813

WONT AND DONE

I have loved; for the first time with passion I rave!
I then was the servant, but now am the slave;
I then was the servant of all:
By this creature so charming I now am fast bound,
To love and love's guerdon she turns all around,
And her my sole mistress I call.
I've had faith; for the first time my faith is now strong!
And though matters go strangely, though matters go wrong,
To the ranks of the faithful I'm true:
Though ofttimes 'twas dark and though ofttimes 'twas drear,
In the pressure of need, and when danger was near,
Yet the dawning of light I now view.
I have eaten; but never have thus relished my food!
For when glad are the senses, and joyous the blood,
At table all else is effaced
As for youth, it but swallows, then whistles an air;
As for me, to a jovial resort Ied repair,
Where to eat, and enjoy what I taste.
I have drunk; but have never thus relished the bowl!
For wine makes us lords, and enlivens the soul,
And loosens the trembling slave's tongue.
Let's not seek to spare then the heart-stirring drink,
For though in the barrel the old wine may sink,
In its place will fast mellow the young.
I have danced, and to dancing am pledged by a vow!
Though no caper or waltz may be raved about now,
In a dance that's becoming, whirl round.
And he who a nosegay of flowers has dressed,
And cares not for one any more than the rest,
With a garland of mirth is aye crowned.
Then once more be merry, and banish all woes!

For he who but gathers the blossoming rose.
By its thorns will be tickled alone.
To-day still, as yesterday, glimmers the star;
Take care from all heads that hang down to keep far,
And make but the future thine own.

1813

TO THE DISTANT ONE

And have I lost thee evermore?
Hast thou, oh fair one, from me flown?
Still in mine ear sounds, as of yore,
Thine every word, thine every tone.
As when at morn the wanderer's eye
Attempts to pierce the air in vain,
When, hidden in the azure sky,
The lark high over him chaunts his strain:
So do I cast my troubled gaze
Through bush, through forest, over the lea;
Thou art invoked by all my lays;
Oh, come then, loved one, back to me!

1789

SPIRIT SONG OVER THE WATERS

The soul of man
Resembleth water:
From heaven it cometh,
To heaven it soareth.
And then again
To earth descendeth,
Changing ever.
Down from the lofty
Rocky wall
Streams the bright flood,
Then spreadeth gently
In cloudy billows
Over the smooth rock,
And welcomed kindly,
Veiling, on roams it,
Soft murmuring,
Toward the abyss.
Cliffs projecting
Oppose its progress, –
Angrily foams it
Down to the bottom,
Step by step.
Now, in flat channel,
Through the meadowland steals it,
And in the polished lake
Each constellation
Joyously peepeth.
Wind is the loving
Wooer of waters;
Wind blends together
Billows all-foaming.

Spirit of man,
Thou art like unto water!
Fortune of man,
Thou art like unto wind!

1789

THE MAGIC NET

Do I see a contest yonder?
See I miracles or pastimes?
Beauteous urchins, five in number,
'Gainst five sisters fair contending, –
Measured is the time they're beating –
At a bright enchantress' bidding.
Glittering spears by some are wielded,
Threads are others nimbly twining,
So that in their snares, the weapons
One would think, must needs be captured,
Soon, in truth, the spears are prisoned;
Yet they, in the gentle war-dance,
One by one escape their fetters
In the row of loops so tender,
That make haste to seize a free one
Soon as they release a captive.
So with contests, strivings, triumphs,
Flying now, and now returning,
Is an artful net soon woven,
In its whiteness like the snow-flakes,
That, from light amid the darkness,
Draw their streaky lines so varied,
As even colours scarce can draw them.
Who shall now receive that garment
Far beyond all others wished-for?
Whom our much-loved mistress favour
As her own acknowledged servant?
I am blest by kindly Fortune's
Tokens true, in silence prayed for!
And I feel myself held captive,
To her service now devoted.

Yet, even while I, thus enraptured,
Thus adorned, am proudly wand'ring,
See! yon wantons are entwining,
Void of strife, with secret ardour,
Other nets, each fine and finer,
Threads of twilight interweaving,
Moonbeams sweet, night-violets' balsam.
Ere the net is noticed by us,
Is a happier one imprisoned,
Whom we, one and all, together
Greet with envy and with blessings.

1803

MY GODDESS

Say, which Immortal
Merits the highest reward?
With none contend I,
But I will give it
To the aye-changing,
Ever-moving
Wondrous daughter of Jove.
His best-beloved offspring.
Sweet Phantasy.
For unto her
Hath he granted
All the fancies which erst
To none allowed he
Saving himself;
Now he takes his pleasure
In the mad one.
She may, crowned with roses,
With staff twined round with lilies,
Roam thro' flowery valleys,
Rule the butterfly-people,
And soft-nourishing dew
With bee-like lips
Drink from the blossom:
Or else she may
With fluttering hair
And gloomy looks
Sigh in the wind
Round rocky cliffs,
And thousand-hued.
Like morn and even.
Ever changing,

Like moonbeam's light,
To mortals appear.
Let us all, then,
Adore the Father!
The old, the mighty,
Who such a beauteous
Never-fading spouse
Deigns to accord
To perishing mortals!
To us alone
Doth he unite her,
With heavenly bonds,
While he commands her,
in joy and sorrow,
As a true spouse
Never to fly us.
All the remaining
Races so poor
Of life-teeming earth.
In children so rich.
Wander and feed
In vacant enjoyment,
And 'mid the dark sorrows
Of evanescent
Restricted life, –
Bowed by the heavy
Yoke of Necessity.
But unto us he
Hath his most versatile,
Most cherished daughter
Granted, – what joy!
Lovingly greet her
As a beloved one!
Give her the woman's
Place in our home!

And oh, may the aged
Stepmother Wisdom
Her gentle spirit
Never seek to harm!
Yet know I her sister,
The older, sedater,
Mine own silent friend;
Oh, may she never,
Till life's lamp is quenched,
Turn away from me, –
That noble inciter,
Comforter, – Hope!

1781

PROMETHEUS

Cover thy spacious heavens, Zeus,
With clouds of mist,
And, like the boy who lops
The thistles' heads,
Disport with oaks and mountain-peaks,
Yet thou must leave
My earth still standing;
My cottage too, which was not raised by thee;
Leave me my hearth,
Whose kindly glow
By thee is envied.
I know nought poorer
Under the sun, than ye gods!
Ye nourish painfully,
With sacrifices
And votive prayers,
Your majesty:
Ye would even starve,
If children and beggars
Were not trusting fools.
While yet a child
And ignorant of life,
I turned my wandering gaze
Up toward the sun, as if with him
There were an ear to hear my wailings,
A heart, like mine,
To feel compassion for distress.
Who helped me
Against the Titans' insolence?
Who rescued me from certain death,
From slavery?

Didst thou not do all this thyself,
My sacred glowing heart?
And glowedst, young and good,
Deceived with grateful thanks
To yonder slumbering one?
I honour thee! and why?
Hast thou ever lightened the sorrows
Of the heavy laden?
Hast thou ever dried up the tears
Of the anguish-stricken?
Was I not fashioned to be a man
By omnipotent Time,
And by eternal Fate,
Masters of me and thee?
Didst thou ever fancy
That life I should learn to hate,
And fly to deserts,
Because not all
My blossoming dreams grew ripe?
Here sit I, forming mortals
After my image;
A race resembling me,
To suffer, to weep,
To enjoy, to be glad,
And thee to scorn,
As I!

1773

From *FAUST*

PROLOGUE IN HEAVEN

THE ARCHANGELS' SONG

RAPHAEL

The sun still chaunts, as in old time,
With brother-spheres in choral song,
And with his thunder-march sublime
Moves his predestined course along.
Strength find the angels in his sight,
Though he by none may fathomed be;
Still glorious is each work of might
As when first formed in majesty.

GABRIEL

And swift and swift, in wondrous guise,
Revolves the earth in splendour bright,
The radiant hues of Paradise
Alternating with deepest night.
From out the gulf against the rock,
In spreading billows foams the ocean, –
And cliff and sea with mighty shock,
The spheres whirl round in endless motion.

MICHAEL

And storms in emulation growl
From land to sea, from sea to land,
And fashion, as they wildly howl,

A circling, wonder-working band.
Destructive flames in mad career
Precede Thy thunders on their way;
Yet, Lord, Thy messengers revere
The soft mutations of Thy day.

THE THREE

Strength find the angels in Thy sight,
Though none may hope to fathom Thee;
Still glorious are Thy works of might,
As when first formed in majesty.

From *ELEGIES*

PART II

ALEXIS AND DORA

Farther and farther away, alas! at each moment the vessel
Hastens, as onward it glides, cleaving the foam-covered flood!
Long is the track ploughed up by the keel where dolphins are
                                        sporting,
Following fast in its rear, while it seems flying pursuit.
All forebodes a prosperous voyage; the sailor with calmness
Leans 'gainst the sail, which alone all that is needed performs.
Forward presses the heart of each seamen, like colours and
                                        streamers;
Backward one only is seen, mournfully fixed near the mast,
While on the blue tinged mountains, which fast are receding,
                                        he gazeth,
And as they sink in the sea, joy from his bosom departs.
Vanished from thee, too, oh Dora, is now the vessel that robs
                                        thee
Of thine Alexis, thy friend, – ah, thy betrothed as well!
Thou, too, art after me gazing in vain. Our hearts are still
                                        throbbing,
Though, for each other, yet ah! 'gainst one another no more.
Oh, thou single moment, wherein I found life! thou
                                        outweighest
Every day which had else coldly from memory fled.
'Twas in that moment alone, the last, that upon me descended
Life, such as deities grant, though thou perceivedest it not.
Phoebus, in vain with thy rays dost thou clothe the ether in
                                        glory:
Thine all-brightening day hateful alone is to me.

Into myself I retreat for shelter, and there, in the silence,
Strive to recover the time when she appeared with each day.
Was it possible beauty like this to see, and not feel it?
Worked not those heavenly charms even on a mind dull as
thine?
Blame not thyself, unhappy one! Oft doth the bard an enigma
Thus propose to the throng, skillfully hidden in words.
Each one enjoys the strange commingling of images graceful,
Yet still is wanting the word which will discover the sense.
When at length it is found, the heart of each hearer is
gladdened,
And in the poem he sees meaning of twofold delight.
Wherefore so late didst thou remove the bandage, oh Amor,
Which thou hadst placed over mine eyes, – wherefore remove
it so late?
Long did the vessel, when laden, lie waiting for favouring
breezes,
'Till in kindness the wind blew from the land over the sea.
Vacant times of youth! and vacant dreams of the future!
Ye all vanish, and nought, saving the moment, remains.
Yes! it remains, – my joy still remains! I hold thee; my Dora,
And thine image alone, Dora, by hope is disclosed.
Oft have I seen thee go, with modesty clad, to the temple,
While thy mother so dear solemnly went by thy side.
Eager and nimble thou wert, in bearing thy fruit to the market,
Boldly the pail from the well didst thou sustain on thy head.
Then was revealed thy neck, then seen thy shoulders so
beauteous,
Then, before all things, the grace filling thy motions was seen.
Oft have I feared that the pitcher perchance was in danger of
falling,
Yet it ever remained firm on the circular cloth.
Thus, fair neighbour, yes, thus I oft was wont to observe thee,
As on the stars I might gaze, as I might gaze on the moon,
Glad indeed at the sight, yet feeling within my calm bosom

Not the remotest desire ever to call them mine own.
Years thus fleeted away! Although our houses were only
Twenty paces apart, yet I thy threshold never crossed.
Now by the fearful flood are we parted! Thou liest to Heaven,
Billow! thy beautiful blue seems to me dark as the night.
All were now in movement; a boy to the house of my father
Ran at full speed and exclaimed: "Hasten thee quick to the
                                             strand
Hoisted the sail is already, even now in the wind it is fluttering,
While the anchor they weigh, heaving it up from the sand;
Come, Alexis, oh come!" – My worthy stout-hearted father
Pressed, with a blessing, his hand down on my curly-locked
                                             head,
While my mother carefully reached me a newly-made bundle,
"Happy mayst thou return!" cried they – "both happy and
                                             rich!"
Then I sprang away, and under my arm held the bundle,
Running along by the wall. Standing I found thee hard by,
At the door of thy garden. Thou smilingly saidst then "Alexis!
Say, are yon boisterous crew going thy comrades to be?
Foreign coasts will thou visit, and precious merchandise
                                             purchase,
Ornaments meet for the rich matrons who dwell in the town.
Bring me, also, I praythee, a light chain; gladly I'll pay thee,
Oft have I wished to possess some stich a trinket as that."
There I remained, and asked, as merchants are wont, with
                                             precision
After the form and the weight which thy commission should
                                             have.
Modest, indeed, was the price thou didst name! I meanwhile
                                             was gazing
On thy neck which deserved ornaments worn but by queens.
Loudly now rose the cry from the ship; then kindly thou
                                             spakest
"Take, I entreat thee, some fruit out of the garden, my friend

Take the ripest oranges, figs of the whitest; the ocean
Beareth no fruit, and, in truth, 'tis not produced by each land."
So I entered in. Thou pluckedst the fruit from the branches,
And the burden of gold was in thine apron upheld.
Oft did I cry, Enough! But fairer fruits were still falling
Into the hand as I spake, ever obeying thy touch.
Presently didst thou reached the arbour; there lay there a
                                                      basket,
Sweet blooming myrtle trees waved, as we drew nigh, over our
                                                      heads.
Then thou beganest to arrange the fruit with skill and in
                                                      silence:
First the orange, which lay heavy as though 'twere of gold,
Then the yielding fig, by the slightest pressure disfigured,
And with myrtle the gift soon was both covered and graced.
But I raised it not up. I stood. Our eyes met together,
And my eyesight grew dim, seeming obscured by a film,
Soon I felt thy bosom on mine! Mine arm was soon twining
Round thy beautiful form; thousand times kissed I thy neck.
On my shoulder sank thy head; thy fair arms, encircling,
Soon rendered perfect the ring knitting the rapturous pair.
Amor's hands I felt: he pressed us together with ardour,
And, from the firmament clear, thrice did it thunder; then tears
Streamed from mine eyes in torrents, thou weptest, I wept,
                                                      both were weeping,
And, 'mid our sorrow and bliss, even the world seemed to die.
Louder and louder they called from the strand; my feet would
                                                      no longer
Bear my weight, and I cried: – "Dora! and art thou not mine?"
"Thine forever!" thou gently didst say. Then the tears we were
                                                      shedding
Seemed to be wiped from our eyes, as by the breath of a god.
Nearer was heard the cry "Alexis!" The stripling who sought
                                                      me
Suddenly peeped through the door. How he the basket

snatched up!

How he urged me away! how pressed I thy hand! Wouldst thou
ask me
How the vessel I reached? Drunken I seemed, well I know.
Drunken my shipmates believed me, and so had pity upon me;
And as the breeze drove us on, distance the town soon
obscured.
"Thine for ever!" thou, Dora, didst murmur; it fell on my
senses
With the thunder of Zeus! while by the thunderer's throne
Stood his daughter, the Goddess of Love; the Graces were
standing
Close by her side! so the bond beareth an impress divine!
Oh then hasten, thou ship, with every favouring zephyr!
Onward, thou powerful keel, cleaving the waves as they foam!
Bring me unto the foreign harbour, so that the goldsmith
May in his workshop prepare straightway the heavenly pledge!
Ay, of a truth, the chain shall indeed be a chain, oh my Dora!
Nine times encircling thy neck, loosely around it entwined
Other and manifold trinkets I'll buy thee; gold-mounted
bracelets,
Richly and skillfully wrought, also shall grace thy fair hand.
There shall the ruby and emerald vie, the sapphire so lovely
Be to the jacinth opposed, seeming its foil; while the gold
Holds all the jewels together, in beauteous union commingled.
Oh, how the bridegroom exults, when he adorns his
betrothed!
Pearls if I see, of thee they remind me; each ring that is shown
me
Brings to my mind thy fair hand's graceful and tapering form.
I will barter and buy; the fairest of all shalt thou choose thee,
Joyously would I devote all of the cargo to thee.
Yet not trinkets and jewels alone is thy loved one procuring;
With them he brings thee whatever gives to a housewife
delight.

Fine and woollen coverlets, wrought with an edging of purple,
Fit for a couch where we both, lovingly, gently may rest;
Costly pieces of linen. Thou sittest and sewest, and clothest
Me, and thyself, and, perchance, even a third with it too.
Visions of hope, deceive ye my heart! Ye kindly Immortals,
Soften this fierce-raging flame, wildly pervading my breast!
Yet how I long to feel them again, those rapturous torments.
When, in their stead, care draws nigh, coldly and fearfully
          calm.
Neither the Furies' torch, nor the hounds of hell with their
          harking
Awe the delinquent so much, down in the plains of despair,
As by the motionless spectre I'm awed, that shows me the fair
          one
Far away: of a truth, open the garden-door stands!
And another one cometh! For him the fruit, too, is falling,
And for him, also, the fig strengthening honey doth yield!
Doth she entice him as well to the arbour? He follows? Oh,
          make me
Blind, ye Immortals! efface visions like this from my mind!
Yes, she is but a maiden! And she who to one doth so quickly
Yield, to another ere long, doubtless, Will turn herself round.
Smile not, Zeus, for this once, at an oath so cruelly broken!
Thunder more fearfully! Strike! – Stay – thy fierce lightnings
          withhold!
Hurl at me thy quivering bolt! In the darkness of midnight
Strike with thy lightning this mast, make it a pitiful wreck!
Scatter the planks all around, and give to the boisterous billows
All these wares, and let me be to the dolphins a prey
Now, ye Muses, enough! In vain would ye strive to depicture
How, in a love-laden breast, anguish alternates with bliss.
Ye cannot heal the wounds, it is true, that love hath inflicted;
Yet from you only proceeds, kindly ones, comfort and balm.

1796

ARTS, PAINTING, SCULPTURE

The Art of Andy Goldsworthy: Complete Works
Andy Goldsworthy: Touching Nature
Andy Goldsworthy in Close-Up
Andy Goldsworthy: Pocket Guide
Andy Goldsworthy In America
Land Art: A Complete Guide

The Art of Richard Long: Complete Works
Richard Long: Pocket Guide
Land Art In the UK
Land Art in Close-Up
Land Art In the U.S.A.
Land Art: Pocket Guide

Installation Art in Close-Up
Minimal Art and Artists In the 1960s and After
Colourfield Painting
Land Art DVD, TV documentary
Andy Goldsworthy DVD, TV documentary
The Erotic Object: Sexuality in Sculpture From Prehistory to the Present Day
Sex in Art: Pornography and Pleasure in Painting and Sculpture
Postwar Art
Sacred Gardens: The Garden in Myth, Religion and Art
Glorification: Religious Abstraction in Renaissance and 20th Century Art
Early Netherlandish Painting
Leonardo da Vinci
Piero della Francesca
Giovanni Bellini
Fra Angelico: Art and Religion in the Renaissance

Mark Rothko: The Art of Transcendence
Frank Stella: American Abstract Artist
Jasper Johns
Brice Marden

Alison Wilding: The Embrace of Sculpture
Vincent van Gogh: Visionary Landscapes
Eric Gill: Nuptials of God
Constantin Brancusi: Sculpting the Essence of Things
Max Beckmann
Caravaggio
Gustave Moreau
Egon Schiele: Sex and Death In Purple Stockings
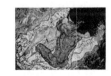
Delizioso Fotografico Fervore: Works In Process 1
Sacro Cuore: Works In Process 2
The Light Eternal: J.M.W. Turner
The Madonna Glorified: Karen Arthurs

LITERATURE

J.R.R. Tolkien: The Books, The Films, The Whole Cultural Phenomenon
J.R.R. Tolkien: Pocket Guide
Tolkien's Heroic Quest
The *Earthsea* Books of Ursula Le Guin
Beauties, Beasts and Enchantment: Classic French Fairy Tales
German Popular Tales by the Brothers Grimm
Philip Ullman and *His Dark Materials*
Sexing Hardy: Thomas Hardy and Feminism
Thomas Hardy's *Tess of the d'Urbervilles*
Thomas Hardy's *Jude the Obscure*
Thomas Hardy: The Tragic Novels
Love and Tragedy: Thomas Hardy
The Poetry of Landscape in Hardy
Wessex Revisited: Thomas Hardy and John Cowper Powys
Wolfgang Iser: Essays and Interviews
Petrarch, Dante and the Troubadours
Maurice Sendak and the Art of Children's Book Illustration
Andrea Dworkin
Cixous, Irigaray, Kristeva: The *Jouissance* of French Feminism
Julia Kristeva: Art, Love, Melancholy, Philosophy, Semiotics and Psychoanalysis
Hélene Cixous I Love You: The *Jouissance* of Writing
Luce Irigaray: Lips, Kissing, and the Politics of Sexual Difference
Peter Redgrove: Here Comes the Flood
Peter Redgrove: Sex-Magic-Poetry-Cornwall
Lawrence Durrell: Between Love and Death, East and West
Love, Culture & Poetry: Lawrence Durrell
Cavafy: Anatomy of a Soul
German Romantic Poetry: Goethe, Novalis, Heine, Hölderlin
Feminism and Shakespeare
Shakespeare: Love, Poetry & Magic
The Passion of D.H. Lawrence .
D.H. Lawrence: Symbolic Landscapes
D.H. Lawrence: Infinite Sensual Violence
Rimbaud: Arthur Rimbaud and the Magic of Poetry
The Ecstasies of John Cowper Powys
Sensualism and Mythology: The Wessex Novels of John Cowper Powys
Amorous Life: John Cowper Powys and the Manifestation of Affectivity (H.W. Fawkner)
Postmodern Powys: New Essays on John Cowper Powys (Joe Boulter)
Rethinking Powys: Critical Essays on John Cowper Powys
Paul Bowles & Bernardo Bertolucci
Rainer Maria Rilke
Joseph Conrad: *Heart of Darkness*
In the Dim Void: Samuel Beckett
Samuel Beckett Goes into the Silence
André Gide: Fiction and Fervour
Jackie Collins and the Blockbuster Novel
Blinded By Her Light: The Love-Poetry of Robert Graves
The Passion of Colours: Travels In Mediterranean Lands
Poetic Forms

POETRY

Ursula Le Guin: Walking In Cornwall
Peter Redgrove: Here Comes The Flood
Peter Redgrove: Sex-Magic-Poetry-Cornwall
Dante: Selections From the *Vita Nuova*

Petrarch, Dante and the Troubadours
William Shakespeare: *The Sonnets*
William Shakespeare: Complete Poems
Blinded By Her Light: The Love-Poetry of Robert Graves
Emily Dickinson: Selected Poems
Emily Brontë: Poems
Thomas Hardy: Selected Poems
Percy Bysshe Shelley: Poems
John Keats: Selected Poems

D.H. Lawrence: Selected Poems
Edmund Spenser: Poems
Edmund Spenser: *Amoretti*
John Donne: Poems

Henry Vaughan: Poems
Sir Thomas Wyatt: Poems
Robert Herrick: Selected Poems
Rilke: Space, Essence and Angels in the Poetry of Rainer Maria Rilke
Rainer Maria Rilke: Selected Poems
Friedrich Hölderlin: Selected Poems
Arseny Tarkovsky: Selected Poems
Novalis: *Hymns To the Night*

Paul Verlaine: Selected Poems
Arthur Rimbaud: Selected Poems
Arthur Rimbaud: *A Season in Hell*
Arthur Rimbaud and the Magic of Poetry
D.J. Enright: By-Blows
Jeremy Reed: Brigitte's Blue Heart
Jeremy Reed: Claudia Schiffer's Red Shoes

Gorgeous Little Orpheus
Radiance: New Poems
Crescent Moon Book of Nature Poetry
Crescent Moon Book of Love Poetry
Crescent Moon Book of Mystical Poetry
Crescent Moon Book of Elizabethan Love Poetry
Crescent Moon Book of Metaphysical Poetry
Crescent Moon Book of Romantic Poetry
Pagan America: New American Poetry

MEDIA, CINEMA, FEMINISM and CULTURAL STUDIES

J.R.R. Tolkien: The Books, The Films, The Whole Cultural Phenomenon
J.R.R. Tolkien: Pocket Guide
The *Lord of the Rings* Movies: Pocket Guide
The Cinema of Hayao Miyazaki
Hayao Miyazaki: *Princess Mononoke*: Pocket Movie Guide
Hayao Miyazaki: *Spirited Away*: Pocket Movie Guide
Tim Burton
Ken Russell

Ken Russell: *Tommy*: Pocket Movie Guide
The Ghost Dance: The Origins of Religion
The Peyote Cult
Cixous, Irigaray, Kristeva: The *Jouissance* of French Feminism
Julia Kristeva: Art, Love, Melancholy, Philosophy, Semiotics and Psychoanalysis
Luce Irigaray: Lips, Kissing, and the Politics of Sexual Difference

Hélene Cixous I Love You: The *Jouissance* of Writing
Andrea Dworkin
'Cosmo Woman': The World of Women's Magazines
Women in Pop Music

Discovering the Goddess (Geoffrey Ashe)
The Poetry of Cinema

The Sacred Cinema of Andrei Tarkovsky
Andrei Tarkovsky: Pocket Guide
Andrei Tarkovsky: *Mirror*: Pocket Movie Guide

Andrei Tarkovsky: *The Sacrifice*: Pocket Movie Guide
Walerian Borowczyk: Cinema of Erotic Dreams

Jean-Luc Godard: The Passion of Cinema
Jean-Luc Godard: *Hail Mary*: Pocket Movie Guide
Jean-Luc Godard: *Contempt*: Pocket Movie Guide
Jean-Luc Godard: *Pierrot le Fou*: Pocket Movie Guide

John Hughes and Eighties Cinema
Ferris Bueller's Day Off: Pocket Movie Guide
Jean-Luc Godard: Pocket Guide
The Cinema of Richard Linklater
Liv Tyler: Star In Ascendance
Blade Runner and the Films of Philip K. Dick
Paul Bowles and Bernardo Bertolucci
Media Hell: Radio, TV and the Press
An Open Letter to the BBC
Detonation Britain: Nuclear War in the UK
Feminism and Shakespeare
Wild Zones: Pornography, Art and Feminism
Sex in Art: Pornography and Pleasure in Painting and Sculpture
Sexing Hardy: Thomas Hardy and Feminism

In my view *The Light Eternal* is among the very best of all the material I read on Turner. (Douglas Graham, director of the Turner Museum, Denver, Colorado)

The Light Eternal is a model monograph, an exemplary job. The subject matter of the book is beautifully organised and dead on beam. (Lawrence Durrell)

It is amazing for me to see my work treated with such passion and respect. (Andrea Dworkin)

CRESCENT MOON PUBLISHING
P.O. Box 1312, Maidstone, Kent, ME14 5XU, Great Britain. www.crmoon.com